Love in the Time of Corona

Love in the Time of Corona

*Advice from a Sex Therapist
for Couples in Quarantine*

Diana Wiley, PhD

C4C, LLC
Seattle, Washington

Published by C4C, LLC
6523 California Ave SW
PMB 322
Seattle, WA 98136

Copyright © 2020 by C4C, LLC

Certain names and identifying details have been changed.

ISBN 978-0-932898-99-9 (paperback)

For contact information, visit www.DearDrDiana.com

Praise for
Love in the Time of Corona

Well-written and practical, it's the perfect book for couples who want to pluck something good out of a demanding and dangerous period in world history.
　　—Pepper Schwartz, PhD, professor of sociology and author of *The Normal Bar*

Dr. Diana provides wise, practical, timely suggestions for enhancing relationships and sex at any time—and especially in this time of coronavirus.
　　—Michael Castleman, publisher of greatsexguidance.com and writer of the "All about Sex" blog at psychologytoday.com

A timely book filled with timeless advice on how to navigate sex and relationships in this challenging time—from one of the best sex and relationship therapists I know.
　　—Eli Coleman, PhD, professor and director of the Program in Human Sexuality at the University of Minnesota Medical School

Dr. Diana presents a fresh and unique sexual travelogue for couples under quarantine, guiding them to re-eroticize their love lives and make use of the healing power of sex.
　　—Dudley Danoff, MD, FACS, president and founder of Cedars-Sinai Tower Urology Medical Group and author of *The Ultimate Guide to Male Sexual Health*

Love in the Time of Corona is a complete love and happiness toolkit that will leave couples feeling grateful for this unprecedented time to pause, reflect, and reconnect.

—**Dr. Nancy Sutton Pierce,** health and wellness educator and clinical sexologist

Dr. Diana offers a wonderful antidote to fear and change: the dependable joys and health benefits of consensual, enthusiastic sexual pleasure. Highly recommended!

—**Nina Hartley, RN,** porn star and author of *Nina Hartley's Guide to Total Sex*

Dr. Diana's sexual advice is presented in a fun-loving way, with many practical, nonthreatening couple's exercises. It's a year's worth of sex therapy in one volume!

—**Mark Schoen, PhD,** founder of sexsmartfilms.com

Love in the Time of Corona is the answer for couples to get through the crises presented by forced isolation together.

—**Dr. Ava Cadell,** founder of Loveology University

If you want to stick together while you're stuck together, you need Diana Wiley's *Love in the Time of Corona*. Dr. Diana is the voice of relationship wisdom—mindful, playful, and pleasure-positive!

—**Sheri Winston, CNM, RN,** award-winning author of *Women's Anatomy of Arousal* and *Succulent SexCraft*

Sex therapist and radio host Dr. Diana Wiley has put together a well-stocked tool chest for any quarantining couple hoping to do a bit of relationship repair during these challenging times.

—**Stephen Snyder, MD,** author of *Love Worth Making: How to Have Ridiculously Great Sex in a Long-Lasting Relationship*

During this "corona crisis" Dr. Diana's sage advice is more needed than ever. I heartily recommend this book to anyone who wants to preserve or improve their romantic relationships.
   —**Bradley A. Coates,** author of *Divorce with Decency*

In a warm, compassionate style, Dr. Diana teaches you the best strategies for maintaining or creating a satisfying sex life with yourpartner while sheltering in place, with an emphasis on communication.
   —**Joan Price,** author of *Naked at Our Age*

Dr. Diana has created a timely and actionable guide to enriching relationships during this time of upheaval, with numerous ideas and activities to grow in love and intimacy.
   —**Jessa Zimmerman,** certified sex therapist and author of *Sex without Stress*

You can use Dr. Diana's practical, time- and client-tested exercises and techniques in these uncertain times to strengthen and revitalize how you approach sex and relationships.
   —**L. Lou Paget, AASECT CSE,** author of *How to Be a Great Lover*

If you are suddenly 24/7 with your beloved, this book offers a delightful way to spend your quarantine. The best part is Dr. Diana's celebration of giving and gratitude.
   —**Elizabeth Rae Larson, MS, DHS, LMHC,** director of the Seattle Institute for Sex Therapy, Education and Research

With decades of experience helping couples get their groove back, Dr. Diana is a go-to resource for couples in sexual crisis and quarantine.
—**Jamye Waxman,** sex therapist and author of *How to Break Up With Anyone*

Love in the Time of Corona provides practical guidance on maintaining and even enhancing your relationship with your partner during this pandemic.
—**Dr. Serena McKenzie, ND,** founder of Whole Life Medicine

In this timely gem of a book, Dr. Diana guides couples from all walks of life to create and maintain a robust sex life. Fabulous!
—**Linda De Villers, PhD,** author of *Love Skills: A Fun Upbeat Guide to Sex-cessful Relationships*

Love in the Time of Corona is a sharply focused, compelling exploration of love and sex during a scary and uncertain time.
—**Sheona McDonald,** director of the documentary film *Candice*

An insightful book with useful strategies to help couples connect and thrive during quarantine. Every couple will benefit from following the wonderful guidance of Dr. Diana!
—**Lori Buckley, PsyD, CST,** author of *21 Decisions for Great Sex and A Happy Relationship*

To my husband, Bryan

I wouldn't have missed this for the world!

Contents

Preface

I have always wanted to write a book to share what I have learned in my long career as a sex therapist. I just didn't think it would take a global pandemic to make the book finally become a reality.

But that's what happened. When it became clear in March 2020 that the coronavirus had developed into a full-blown crisis, my husband Bryan and I started talking about ways that we could help. Clients in my sex therapy practice were already worried about an unknown future. As I switched to videoconference sessions with my clients, I began to offer suggestions about how couples could strengthen their connection while quarantined at home. I know—and the research confirms—that having good sex can relieve stress and anxiety.

That was the spark that led to *Love in the Time of Corona*. I have helped a lot of people create more satisfying sex lives, and I wanted to share that information with a wider audience, especially now that millions of couples are enjoying and/or enduring this time of forced togetherness.

I have always been fascinated by sex. My parents, who were exceptional role models for playful passion, displayed a matter-of-fact attitude that did not burden me with feelings of shame about my own sexuality.

I studied sex and relationships in graduate school. I discovered that my knack for talking about sex can put many people at ease. I have continued to learn as much as I can about the topic over the course of my three-decade career as a licensed marriage and family therapist and board-certified sex therapist. I want to never stop opening up people's lives!

Furthermore, my advice to couples is informed and enhanced by my personal journey. I have continued to grow my inner life as I expanded my horizons of possibilities. In my twenties, I enjoyed many travel adventures and sexual encounters before I settled into a track that combined family and career.

I am now a woman in my 70s, in the full ripeness of my years. I have survived loss, learned again how to live alone, and have now created new dreams for myself. After my former husband died suddenly, I spent ten years as a widow before meeting Bryan through Match.com. (Yes, online dating does work!) We have been together since 2010 and we got married in 2018. We are very well matched in terms of our high libidos and sexual skills and interests. We are so glad we found each other!

My own path toward an empowered sense of self and sexual satisfaction brought me life lessons that I integrate into client treatment plans and interventions. I teach that sex can enliven the mind as well as the senses. It helps that I am so sex-positive! I believe that sex is a divine gift, just waiting for each of us to develop and enjoy over the entire span of a lifetime.

I am also a gerontologist, specializing in aging and sexuality. I believe that the older you get, the better you get. Many people strive to reach their full sexual potential early in life, until they find it is more likely to happen in their 40s, 50s, and 60s (or beyond).

Among the many positive aspects of reigniting your relationship in these unusual times is that sex is really good for your health. It is great exercise and it keeps your body functioning well. It's fabulous for your heart, encourages flexibility, and produces more youthful, sexy hormones. Feeling joy from a satisfying sex life is my best cosmetic!

I believe that couples who are living through this phase of increased togetherness have a unique opportunity to live out their sexual ambitions. Yes, you can find inspiration in adversity.

This book is your guide to redream, refresh, and renew your relationship while in quarantine—and beyond. Now that you have more time with your partner, make the most of it!

—Dr. Diana

Acknowledgments

My parents, John and Margaret Steere, were affectionate with each other and with my sister and me. They taught us the Facts of Life, letting us know that sex was a fun, positive aspect of marriage. The secure attachment I experienced with them has enabled me to enjoy adult intimate relationships to the fullest.

My children, Kate and John, have always been supportive of my profession as a sex therapist. Sure, there were some embarrassing moments in their teenage years, but at least I was never a boring mom!

My Grandma Helen offered healthy messages about aging and sexuality, well into her 80s. I once asked her, "When do you think sexual desire ends?" She replied, "I'll let you know."

Dr. Maria Flaherty is a friend, mentor, and wonderful human being. She served as one of my supervisors for licensing as a therapist; later, for seven years we co-led two women's sexuality groups in San Jose.

Dr. Elizabeth Rae Larson, director of the Seattle Institute for Sex Therapy, Education and Research, has been a steady source of support. She leads our consultation groups. Rae is wise and experienced.

Dr. Serena McKenzie, ND, who specializes in sexual medicine, has been a good friend. (She also officiated at our wedding.) Working with her deepened my understanding of the crucial mind-body connection for female sexuality, a powerful concept I first became acquainted with when I worked as a sex therapist at the UCLA Female Sexual Medicine Center.

I met Dr. Stella Resnick at least thirty years ago when she began focusing on the concept of *pleasure*. That was a direction I liked! She is a great friend and mentor. Dr. Stella, who has written three books, also shared her personal secret to getting a book done: *determination*.

I am grateful for my clients who shared their histories and problems with me. They have helped me realize how important sex is to mental and physical health, as well as to overall well-being. I have shared some of their stories in this book (with names and other details changed to protect confidentiality).

Thanks to Leif Utne, who serves as an integral member of our publishing team. Leif's skills at wordsmithing and online media, as well as his extensive knowledge and interest in human sexuality, have helped make this book a timely and useful resource. Thanks also to other members of the production team, including Lindsey Powers Gay, Karyn Wittmeyer, Rhys Hansen, and Hannah Adams.

Most of all, I want to express my gratitude for my husband, Bryan Brewer. He is an excellent writer and he contributed a great deal to the organization and writing of *Love in the Time of Corona*. He has heard my stories over the last ten years, and he has listened well. For a long time, I have wanted to put out a book, and now I am so thankful that Bryan has helped me achieve that goal. We are a fabulous team and I could not have done this without him!

Introduction

He allowed himself to be swayed by his conviction that human
beings are not born once and for all on the day their mothers
give birth to them, but that life obliges them over and over again
to give birth to themselves.

GABRIEL GARCÍA MÁRQUEZ, LOVE IN THE TIME OF CHOLERA

As I write these words in early May 2020, the spring
flowers here in Seattle, Washington are joyously
popping up in a profusion of vibrant colors. They
remind me of the promise of rebirth, of the regular and
dependable cycle of the seasons.

Yet spring this year is unlike any other we have experienced
in our lifetimes. Instead of fun gatherings with friends to
celebrate the return of warm weather, we are sequestered at
home—by government order—to help slow down the spread
of the coronavirus.

The world has been transformed. The arrival of this
pandemic has overtaken our lives with unexpected speed and
urgency. Social distancing is the only effective public health
response we have that can "flatten the curve" and prevent our
healthcare system from being overwhelmed with grievously ill
patients. Although most people who become infected with this
respiratory virus will recover, the COVID-19 disease it causes
has already killed hundreds of thousands worldwide,

especially older folks and those with underlying health conditions.

This pandemic brings many uncertainties. We don't know how long required social distancing will continue, or even if our society will need to engage in several waves of preventative distancing over the coming months (and years?). You don't know if you—or a loved one—will get the disease and possibly die. You may have lost your job and feel anxious about your financial survival. You may be concerned about getting access to medical treatment if hospitals and healthcare workers are inundated with patients. You may be worried about the long-term economic impact on your career, your business, or your retirement fund. The list goes on.

Indeed, these are uncertain times. Your concerns and questions are valid, but unfortunately, few definitive answers are available. This level of uncertainty can lead to increased stress and anxiety. It can test your resilience in the face of the unknown.

Compounding the stress and anxiety is being confined to home for an indefinite time. Fortunately, you can go out for essential tasks, such as grocery shopping and medical appointments, but the clear guideline is otherwise "Stay home, stay healthy."

If you are in quarantine with family members, the social friction normal in many relationships can be greatly amplified by prolonged periods of being cooped up together. This is especially true if you have children at home, too.

These conditions can produce significant challenges for maintaining your mental health. As a licensed marriage and family therapist, I am concerned about the potential for discord and distress that can devastate couples in quarantine.

For more than thirty years I have had a front row seat to the trials and tribulations of numerous couples within my therapy practice, and I know that even the healthiest relationships can become strained under the current conditions.

I am also a board-certified sex therapist, having helped many of those same couples resolve their sexual issues and enjoy happier relationships. I have been privileged to witness many clients experience the healing benefits of finding more sexual pleasure and intimacy together.

Therein lies the essence of my main message in this book: *enjoyable sexual activity between partners can distinctly benefit a couple's mental and physical health.*

Maintaining a healthy relationship with your partner is even more critical in these extraordinary times. I'm here to encourage you and your partner to make the most of this extended period of "forced togetherness." Use it as an opportunity to explore your sexual relationship and rekindle the sparks of passion. In addition to having fun, you may discover deeper levels of intimacy, both with your partner and within yourself.

You are also likely to experience some of the many proven health benefits of sexual activity. In particular, numerous studies of various populations have shown that having more pleasurable sex reduces stress and eases anxiety. Plus, it is great cardio exercise that burns calories!

As a couple in quarantine, you can use sex as an effective stress-relief strategy that is right at your fingertips (literally!). As my husband and I like to say: "It's fun, it's free, and it's the fountain of youth."

My Advice to You

I've arranged this book around ten strategies that have proven valuable to my clients over the years. I've chosen tips that I think are especially useful for couples in quarantine.

Here's a quick summary to help you focus on which ones have the most appeal for you and your partner.

Chapter 1: Get to Know Your Partner Better

Do you know what your partner really wants? Does your partner know what you really want? Try some of these exercises to improve your communication and discover new things about your partner's sexual and relationship preferences. You might be surprised at what you learn…and it could lead to more interesting and satisfying sex.

Chapter 2: Plan Your Date Night at Home

It's so easy to miss out on the benefits of having sex by simply letting the time slip by. Set a reminder on the calendar and plan your date night at home. Sex does not have to be spontaneous. Planning for romance and passion is the best approach to make it happen!

Chapter 3: Be Mindful about Sex

Mindfulness is a deceptively simple technique you can apply in many areas of your life, including sex. I have suggestions about how you can learn to pay better attention during sexual activity, which can lead to more arousal, pleasure, and satisfaction.

Chapter 4: Use Touch to Relieve Stress

Touch is a powerful tool for soothing tension, but it can also be an irritant when in prolonged close quarters with your partner. I give some guidelines for more intentional and thoughtful touching during the day. I also suggest several sensual touch exercises to help couples who have been "out of touch" gradually reengage in sexual and nonsexual ways.

Chapter 5: Revitalize Your Senses

Despite the steady influx of information from TV or the internet, being stuck at home in the same environment can gradually dull your senses and lead to boredom. I have suggestions for sensory and sensual activities that can help you feel more alive.

Chapter 6: Laugh and Play Together

In my view, learning to be playful at times during sex is a key to increased satisfaction. (There's a good reason the activity leading up to intercourse is called "fore*play*!") I share some ideas about how to successfully engage in fun and playful activities with your partner.

Chapter 7: Try Something New

Novelty—enjoying something new and different—stimulates the release of the neurotransmitter dopamine, which in turn fosters desire and arousal. It's central to the experience of being "turned on." This chapter suggests a myriad of ways you can introduce novelty into your lovemaking.

Chapter 8: Learn More about Sex

Did you know that people who have more sexual knowledge are also more confident in their sexual conduct? A confident partner is a huge turn-on for many people. I'll guide you to trusted resources you can take advantage of while you and your partner are in quarantine.

Chapter 9: Express Gratitude

The mere act of expressing gratitude provides many benefits for your physical and emotional health. Taking the time to say what you are thankful for about your partner also builds trust, which can help you more easily surrender to the ecstasy of sexual passion.

Chapter 10: Recommit to Your Relationship

In these uncertain times, your values about your life and your relationship can come into sharper focus. Rather than ruminate on potential catastrophe, intentionally connect with your partner and find ways to strengthen the physical, emotional, and spiritual bonds between you.

Bonus Chapter Available Online: Cannabis for Couples

More than thirty states in the United States have legalized some form of cannabis (marijuana), either for medical or recreational purposes. Did you know that cannabis, when used properly, can heighten your enjoyment of sex in a number of ways? It's not for everyone. But for those who are curious, I give some guidance on how you can use cannabis to boost pleasure and intimacy in your relationship. Get the free download at www.DearDrDiana.com.

I hope that you will find the information in this book helpful as you and your partner navigate the stress accompanying quarantine during this global crisis. The issues that confront us on a daily basis are serious and highly consequential. I don't in any way mean to diminish the importance of dealing with these critical problems.

I just know from my decades of helping clients (and from my own personal experience) that having healthy sex with a committed partner is an excellent way to reduce tension and alleviate anxieties, both of which may be much more pronounced now. Even after the stress of quarantine subsides, these tips provide valuable guidance about how you can improve your relationship over time.

Some people have called me a "cheerleader for great sex," and I wholeheartedly embrace that attitude. I hope you will, too.

Chapter 1
Get to Know Your Partner Better

People change and forget to tell each other.

LILLIAN HELLMAN

How well do you really know your partner? If you've been quarantined together for at least a few weeks, I'm willing to bet that you've learned some things about them that you didn't know before.

Maybe she tells the same story multiple times to her friends on the phone and you are annoyed by the way she changes certain details each time. Perhaps you are frustrated when he tries to hide his furtive video game playing on his phone. Maybe you are delighted to discover she has been putting money aside each month to save for a dream vacation for the two of you. Perhaps you learn that he washes out the garbage bin every week to keep it from stinking. This blossoming of intimate little discoveries is happening for millions of couples all over the world.

While you are adapting to each other's personal habits during quarantine, you could also use this unusual time as an opportunity to learn more useful information about your partner—information that could benefit your relationship and deepen your sense of intimacy and connection over the long haul. Sometimes you have to do a little digging to get to the heart of the matter.

That was the case for Sarah and Frederick, a middle-aged couple each now on their second marriage. He was beginning to struggle with erectile dysfunction, and the prospect of not being able to have intercourse worried them both. This was the main way that they enjoyed sex with each other. An examination by a urologist revealed no underlying physical problems, but taking ED medications helped only once in a while.

I suggested to Sarah and Frederick that they try the Sex Menu exercise, where each expresses their interest, or lack of interest, in a wide variety of intimate activities. (The exercise and the menu list are included at the end of this chapter.) My goal was to get them thinking about other sexual activities—what I call "outercourse"—they might enjoy that did not require Frederick to have an erection. We discussed details on their lists and looked for some areas of common interest.

Sarah pointed out that Frederick had noted on his menu that he was interested in having her wear lingerie and engage in naughty sex talk, something they had never discussed or done before. It turned out this was a secret fantasy of his, but he had felt too embarrassed to bring it up. They had been married for only three years and because he feared rejection, he had buried the notion in his mind, thinking there was no possibility Sarah would be interested. Well, Sarah *was* interested, especially if the activity could have a positive effect on her husband's erections. I encouraged them to pursue this, to talk in more detail, to try out some scenarios, and give each other feedback. It didn't take long before Frederick's arousal came thundering back, and they both started enjoying more frequent and vigorous sex together. Using the Sex Menu, they discovered some new and exciting activities that revitalized their sex life and deepened their connection!

This chapter covers several very different exercises you can do together to learn more about each other. Among the many suggestions I have given couples over the years, these exercises have had the greatest positive impact.

Some Simple Ways to Connect

First, I would like to offer two simple exercises that you can use to deepen your connection with your partner. The Deep Listening exercise encourages you to really understand what your partner is trying to communicate. This can be particularly helpful in resolving disputes. It's designed to not only hone your listening skills, but also to bolster feelings of empathy for your partner.

The Eye Gazing exercise helps you connect nonverbally using only your eyes. It's a wonderful way to learn how to be more vulnerable in your relationship, which can bring the two of you closer together. Furthermore, a number of clients who practice eye gazing have told me that they experience new realms of knowledge—you might even say spiritual knowledge—about their innermost selves.

Deep Listening Exercise

A big factor in good communication within a couple is the ability to listen well. A typical conversation strategy—which we usually do unconsciously—is to "listen to respond." In other words, as you listen to a person talk, you are already forming your thoughts about what you will say in response. Most people can relate to this, at least some of the time. It can be especially prevalent in conversations with loved ones. You know their stories and it's easy to anticipate what you *think* they are saying.

But listening to respond usually interferes with your ability to really *understand* what your partner is saying. (That's why arguments are euphemistically called *mis*understandings.) The Deep Listening exercise helps reduce negative interactions and can lead to more agreeable solutions.

This exercise, which is inspired by the tradition of the "talking stick" used by native and aboriginal cultures, particularly in the Pacific Northwest and West Africa, uses a ritual object to denote which speaker "has the floor," that is, the person who has the right to speak without being interrupted. Although traditionally used in group settings, the Deep Listening exercise has been adapted for effective use by a couple. Here's how it works:

1. Agree on the single topic of discussion and stay on track. Going off-topic dilutes the effectiveness of this exercise. Stay focused and don't bring up extraneous issues.

2. Choose an item to serve as the "talking object" for this exercise. It can be pretty much any item you agree on, such as a pen or pencil, as long as you can hold it in one hand and easily pass it to your partner.

3. Decide who goes first. Hold the talking object while you speak. Share your thoughts and feelings about the issue at hand. No interruptions—only the person holding the object talks. When you are finished, pass the object to your partner.

Your partner thanks you for sharing and then might also ask you to clarify any details about what you said, and then passes the talking object back to you.

4. You provide any clarification requested and pass the object back to your partner. Repeat this clarification interchange as necessary.

5. Then your partner tells you what they heard you say (this is the crux of the exercise) and passes the object back to you.

6. You give feedback on whether or not you think your partner understood you.

7. Together, keep going back and forth until you are satisfied that your partner understands what you want to communicate.

8. Then your partner takes a turn and you repeat the process until you both feel that you have been understood.

9. Remember, only the person holding the talking object talks.

One of the key benefits of this method is that it may help you feel that you have been heard and understood. It slows down your communication into discrete steps so that each of you can focus on really listening to your partner.

You can use the Deep Listening exercise as often as you like. And it doesn't have to be focused on misunderstandings. It's actually a very powerful method to articulate deeply held feelings that you want your partner to better understand, or that you want to better understand yourself. If you value clear communication with your partner, I encourage you to find creative ways to apply the deep listening exercise together.

Eye Gazing Exercise

This simple exercise takes only about five minutes. It's an excellent way to maintain your connection as you navigate the many demands of life during quarantine with your partner.

The purpose of this exercise is to deepen intimacy. At first it may seem quite uncomfortable and you may have difficulty maintaining your silent gaze for very long. Don't worry; that's a normal reaction if you're new to this. It takes practice, but your reward may be more meaningful insights into yourself, your partner, and your relationship. Here's how to do this exercise:

1. Sit comfortably facing each other with your knees touching so that you can easily see your partner's eyes.

2. Start by closing your eyes and breathing easily and fully into your belly. Notice how your body feels and notice any emotions you might have.

3. Once you feel connected to yourself, open your eyes and gaze into your partner's eyes. If you need a point of focus, direct your attention to just one of your partner's eyes. Let your gaze become soft, blink normally, and stay attuned to your feelings and sensations as you observe your partner.

4. Together, take five slow, full breaths. Allow yourself to feel centered.

5. Breathe at a comfortable level while maintaining nonverbal eye contact. No talking allowed.

6. Continue the eye gazing for five full minutes. It helps to soften the muscles in your face so that your partner can see you fully.

7. If you get distracted and your attention wanders, take a deep breath and bring your focus back to what you are seeing in your partner's eyes. Allow any feelings that arise to show on your face and in your eyes.

8. When the five minutes is over, close your eyes and breathe for a few more moments. Take this time to connect to your own sensations and feelings. Then open your eyes.

9. End the exercise with a hug or some other form of affection.

I encourage you and your partner to talk about your experiences with this exercise. Did you feel comfortable? Did you feel self-conscious? Did you notice the urge to fill up the silence with words? Did you sense a different level of communication with your partner?

Some people who do this exercise become flooded with feelings of awe and gratitude. This is a natural response. The eyes are the windows to the soul, the saying goes. And when you embrace the possibilities of this type of communication, your heart can open. The benefits to your relationship can be profound.

I hope you'll try this Eye Gazing exercise with your partner. It makes a great ritual for the two of you to connect.

Talking About Sex

Many couples have difficulty talking about sex. They become uncomfortable or embarrassed when sexual subjects come up. They often fumble through their sexual activity together because they don't express their feelings, or desires, or what feels good, or what doesn't feel good. This can lead to misunderstandings, crossed signals, and hurt feelings.

There may be a variety of factors that contribute to this reticence. Strict parental attitudes. Religious upbringing and beliefs. Guilt or shame from early sexual experiences. Ignorance of basic anatomy and sexual functioning. Fear of rejection. Self-judgment.

This is so unfortunate, because talking with your partner openly and clearly is a key element of greater sexual fulfillment. I sometimes like to tell clients, *"Don't practice psychic sex."* Don't expect your partner to magically know what you want. Use your words to tell them.

Listening to your partner is equally important. Communication is a two-way street, so you need to hone your skills at both giving and receiving verbal cues.

Learning to talk about sex takes time and practice. If you would like to see some improvement in this area, here are a few suggestions to get started:

- Do the Sex Menu exercise later in this chapter. This will help you get more comfortable with sexual nomenclature, which is essential for good communication. Discuss which sexual words you each like to use in describing your bodies and your sexual activity. Pay attention to particular words that have an extra emotional charge—either positive or negative—and work those words into (or out of) your vocabulary.

- Do the Body Survey exercise in Chapter 4. Talk about each other's sexual anatomy as you discuss what might feel good (or bad) to each of you.

- Do the Full-Body Caressing exercise in Chapter 4. Give specific feedback to your partner as you touch each other intimately in successive stages of arousal (but stopping short of intercourse).

Then, when you do move on to intercourse, oral sex, etc., in the fourth stage of the caressing exercise, continue talking. An easy way to start is to simply describe what is happening, such as "I am now stroking your penis," or "I am now inserting my finger in your vagina." This may seem stilted or awkward at first, and that's OK. You're probably not used to talking about sex when you're having it.

After you've tried this a few times, it should start to seem easier. You can even make it a game of sexual requests, taking turns saying what you want. As you gain some comfort with this kind of dialogue, you may find yourselves using certain words or phrases that work best for you. You may even develop pet names for sexual positions and activities, as well as different body parts ("cock" and "pussy" seem to be the most popular).

Learning to talk with your partner about sex and during sex has several benefits. Most importantly, you give and receive verbal feedback that helps you become better lovers. Listen to your partner and respond accordingly. This allows you to adjust your activity or technique so that you are both getting the pleasure you deserve.

By the same token, I am not suggesting that you talk *all the time* during sex. It can be helpful when getting started and when you need to correct course. But for much of the time you may just want to focus on the feelings in your body or the way your partner looks. Too much talking can keep you in your head, which may cause you to miss out on some sublime pleasures.

Surveys have shown that couples who have open discussions about their sex lives end up having more satisfying sex. Part of the reason has to do with getting information about what positions or practices work best. This makes sex flow more easily. But perhaps an even bigger benefit is the emotional bonding. This kind of sharing builds trust and intimacy, which allows you to be more present with each other in the moment.

Comparing Likes and Dislikes

Especially if you have been together for a long time, you may think that you know everything about what your partner likes and doesn't like about sex. An easy way to find out is to ask. Paths of arousal sometimes change over the years. And you may be surprised by what you discover!

<u>Sex Menu Exercise</u>

That's what the Sex Menu exercise is all about: being explicit about your preferences. The list of items on the menu below is by no means comprehensive. It's just a springboard for discussion. That's why there are some blank lines at the bottom of the list for either partner to add other activities that interests them.

Each partner should fill out their own copy of the menu. For each numbered item, consider whether or not you would be interested in being either the Giver or the Receiver of the activity. Then write a "G" (for Giver) or an "R" (for Receiver) in the appropriate YES, MAYBE, or NO column. For example, item no. 30 is "Spanking." If you would like to give a spanking, write a G in the YES column. If you do not want to receive a spanking, write an R in NO column.

Then share your lists and discuss the similarities and differences. It can be a good way to validate how well you know your partner. It can also highlight discrepancies in your preferences, giving you opportunities to explore and perhaps find compromises. And you just may find some new activities that each of you is interested in trying. Doesn't that sound like fun?

	Varieties of Sexual Behavior	Giver and/or Receiver		
	(Not a comprehensive list)	YES	MAYBE	NO
1	Hugging			
2	Light kissing			
3	Deep kissing			
4	Neck & shoulder rub			
5	Touching breasts with clothes on			
6	Touching buttocks with clothes on			
7	Touching genital area with clothes on			
8	Touching bare breasts			
9	Sucking on nipples			
10	Touching bare buttocks			
11	Touching bare genital area			
12	Stroking vulva			
13	Fingers in vagina			
14	Manual stimulation of clitoris			
15	G-spot stimulation with finger(s)			
16	Mutual masturbation			
17	Cunnilingus			

	Varieties of Sexual Behavior	Giver and/or Receiver		
	(Not a comprehensive list)	YES	MAYBE	NO
18	Stroking penis			
19	Fellatio			
20	Vaginal intercourse			
21	Different positions			
22	Anal play			
23	Anilingus			
24	Anal intercourse			
25	Dildo			
26	Vibrator			
27	Butt plug			
28	Blindfold			
29	Restraints			
30	Spanking			
31	Flogging			
32	Domination			
33	Submission			
34	Role play fantasy			

	Varieties of Sexual Behavior	Giver and/or Receiver		
	(Not a comprehensive list)	YES	MAYBE	NO
35	Dress-up, lingerie, kink attire			
36	Naughty sex talk			
37	Voyeurism			
38	Exhibitionism			
39	Threesomes			
40	Group sex			
41	Fetishes			

The Sex Menu exercise can be quite revealing. You may want to revisit and revise your menus periodically as your preferences evolve over time. That's part of the pleasure of getting to know your partner better.

Chapter 2
Plan Your Date Night at Home

I haven't had sex in so long I've forgotten who ties up who.

JOAN RIVERS

So now you have a lot more time together while you and your partner are in quarantine due to the restrictions imposed by the coronavirus pandemic. One of your first thoughts might be, "Hey, now we can have more sex!"

That's a great thought, because having more sex is a proven stress-reliever. And that's in addition to the fun and pleasure you'll enjoy.

But beware. It can be easy to let the time slip away with mindless activities. You may have good intentions to have more sex, but the ready availability of TV, internet, video games, books, and ever-present phones can suck up your time. Then you're too tired to have sex. "Maybe tomorrow night," you might say. A few days later the pattern repeats. Days and even weeks pass with no sex. Too bad! You're missing opportunities to have fun and to relieve stress and anxiety.

Furthermore, spending your days occupied by a lot of screen time can increase the psychological strain you may feel.

Getting absorbed in the minutiae of the constant news cycle or the latest Facebook memes can sap your energy.

Put Sex on the Calendar

The solution seems easy: talk with your partner, agree on the schedule for your "date night," and then put it on the calendar. You're being intentional and proactive to carve out some time for pleasure and connection.

Sounds simple, right? Well, in my therapy practice over the years, I've suggested to many couples that they schedule a date night. And sometimes I get pushback on this idea from men and women both.

The most common objection is, "Sex should be spontaneous." One of you might feel that scheduling a date night means that the other person's desire is somehow forced or artificial: "If my partner really wants me, then we should fall into each other's arms in a flurry of passion when the moment strikes."

That's a recipe for frustration built on a Hollywood myth. Those "flurry of passion" scenes depicted in the movies are carefully crafted to evoke romantic feelings and fantasies in the viewer. They feel good. They provide a thrill. They sell tickets!

But compared to most of these stories on the screen, real life is usually a lot more mundane. If you wait around for that sudden moment of passion to erupt, you can wait a long time. Plus, the stresses of being in quarantine further diminish the likelihood of such moments. This can lead to growing dissatisfaction for either or both of you.

The absence of spontaneous sex doesn't necessarily mean that your lover doesn't like you or want you. It's just that the logistics of daily life and juggling priorities often means that passion drops down toward the bottom of the list...or even falls completely off the list.

If this description applies to you, I invite you to examine your beliefs about spontaneous sex. Think back to some of the early times when you were exposed to this idea. Can you remember movies, characters, scenes, or stories about this myth of two people magically meeting each other with equal fervor?

These romantic stories may speak to your emotional core. They help stimulate your feelings and desire for intimacy and love. And that's a good thing. But as I said, for most of us these romantic ideals bear little resemblance to real life. The trick is to balance your ideals with the practical realities of your situation.

Recognize that both romance and reality have their advantages, but each at the right time and the right place. If you can move beyond your beliefs—or at least suspend your beliefs long enough to try some date nights at home—you may find that there are many benefits to scheduling sex.

This is what happened with Ricardo and Gabriella, a couple I had been seeing for more than a year. When the pandemic quarantine and social distancing measures went into effect, they got stressed out from being cooped up at home together. Previously, they had spent a fair amount of time apart, with each working long hours at their office jobs. But now they were working from home and the constant togetherness was challenging. They contacted me for a teleconference session to see if I could help.

My first suggestion was for them to agree on some guidelines for daily touch (described in Chapter 4: Use Touch to Relieve Stress). This would ease some of the tension they were feeling from being in prolonged proximity to each other. But I also emphasized that they needed to make sure to maintain some intimate connection. I suggested they schedule some date nights where they could intentionally relax together and be sexual.

Gabriella was reluctant at first, citing the "sex should be spontaneous" mantra. With a little probing she revealed that she had spent a lot of time watching telenovelas and reading romance novels as a young adult. It didn't take too much to convince her that her bias was unfounded. She agreed to give it a try. To her delight, she discovered that she could indeed schedule time for sex and that she really enjoyed those date nights. With a little planning, she and Ricardo were able to defuse the tension between them and enjoy some sexual intimacy as well!

Another objection I hear goes something like this: "What if date night arrives and I am not in the mood?" In other words, "I might not feel like having sex."

Most commonly I hear this from women, and studies have shown that up to a third of women say they lack libido for no apparent reason. In contrast, the vast majority of men often feel desire and are easily aroused.

So how do you deal with this discrepancy? First, let's distinguish between two types of sexual desire. *Spontaneous sexual desire* is just what it sounds like: it arises out of the blue and may or may not be the result of any physical stimulation. Studies have shown that about 75% of men but only about 15% of women experience this type of desire. Gabriella fits within this majority of women, which could explain why she is concerned about not feeling sexual desire when date night arrives. It's not part of her arousal profile.

The second type is *responsive sexual desire*, which, as the name implies, occurs in response to some kind of stimulation, from physical touch to emotional foreplay. Many more women experience this type of desire. In simple terms, they need something to warm them up, some stimulation to jumpstart their engines.

The solution is straightforward: agree to begin with some stimulation first, even though you may not feel the desire just yet. Here's where the more eager partner (usually a man) needs to slow things down. It often takes more time to evoke desire in the partner who is "not in the mood." Start slowly with some leisurely massage. Try some playful, sensual interactions more focused on the whole body. Yes, include the genitals, but don't focus there. Explore the whole body. After a while the desire may catch up with the arousal, which makes for much more satisfying sex for both of you. (For more ideas on how to ease into intimacy, see Chapter 4: Use Touch to Relieve Stress.)

One key to a successful date night at home is having and expressing clear intentions. Take time to communicate and agree on what each of you wants from your date night at home. And then set the date.

If it turns out that one of you is really not in the mood for sex when date night arrives, then give your lover a rain check: a commitment that you will reschedule your date night soon, hopefully after just a day or two.

Before I go on with suggestions for planning your date night at home, I want to say a little about "alone time." Being cooped up in your home with your partner can lead to different reactions, from day to day and from person to person. While I advocate for some intentional time together, it's also important that each partner gets some time alone.

The amount of alone time that works best depends a lot on whether you are an introvert (a person who generally needs more time alone) or an extrovert (who generally needs less time alone). Discuss your preferences with your partner and do what you can to make accommodations for each other. To give your partner some space, go for a walk alone (while maintaining social distancing, of course.) Meditate on the front porch. Work on a project in the garage. Clean out the basement. Go grocery shopping. These are all ways that you can give your partner some time alone.

Another important aspect of alone time is to give your partner the time and space to engage in what is usually a solitary activity: masturbation. Did you know that studies have shown that people who have regular partnered sex tend to masturbate *more* than those who are not partnered?

The fact that your lover may want to masturbate does not necessarily mean that it's a substitute for making love with you. The two activities can actually reinforce each other and lead to more satisfying sex, especially if you are able to talk freely about it. Being able to talk openly and honestly about what's going on sexually with each of you (including masturbation) can lead to deeper intimacy and pleasure.

Develop a Plan

Now that you have written *DATE NIGHT* on the calendar, you may begin to feel some anticipation. Perhaps you start imagining some romantic aspects of your upcoming evening, such as whispers of sweet nothings and other expressions of love and desire from your partner. Maybe you can actually sense what it will feel like to be in your bedroom with clean sheets, scented candles, romantic music, and dim lights. You may begin to get excited about the prospect of having hot, passionate sex.

This is great anticipatory foreplay, but I recommend that you do some planning first so that you both can get the most from your date night.

With your partner, discuss how you would like the evening to unfold. It's a good idea to plan some kind of activity to help the two of you reconnect before you jump into bed. Again, taking it slow will really pay off.

Here are some ideas for activities you can do to make your date night at home an evening of sensual pleasure and enjoyment, all in the service of emotional foreplay:

- Cook a meal together, or order a tasty dinner for takeout or delivery
- Set your dinner table with fresh flowers, candlelight and fine china
- Choose a romantic or sexy movie to watch together
- Give each other a massage or back rub
- Play a board game you both enjoy
- Read poetry or an erotic short story out loud to one another
- Go through old photos and reminisce about shared memories
- Have a pillow fight (but don't be too aggressive)
- Engage in the "Eye Gazing" or "Deep Listening" exercises (described in Chapter 1) to deepen your connection
- Listen to some favorite dance music and move your bodies together
- Have some sensual finger foods handy to feed each other
- Take a bubble bath or shower together
- And so on...

These suggestions may get you thinking about some other enjoyable things you and your partner could do together—

things that may have individual or shared meaning for the two of you.

The idea is to discuss what you want to have happen. Or maybe not: one of you may prefer to surprise the other person. Sometimes a little mystery about an upcoming surprise can trigger the release of dopamine, which may add to the arousal. You could take turns on successive date nights about who plans the evening. There's no right or wrong way to do this. The important thing is to do some planning and preparation so that the experience feels special. Be creative about some ways to pleasantly stimulate your senses (see Chapter 5: Revitalize Your Senses.) Try something new and different (see Chapter 7: Try Something New.) Both of these will add to your overall enjoyment and will heighten your sexual response to each other.

Set the Scene

As you prepare for the evening, pay extra attention to setting the scene for a romantic or sexy time together. Take time to clean the bedroom, especially, but also other rooms in the house where you will spend time on your date, such as the kitchen, living room, or dining room.

Another part of setting the scene is your personal appearance and hygiene. Don't attend your date night at home in the dirty pajamas you have been wearing for days. Make the effort to do your shower/shave/etc. routine before your date. Put on some nice clothes. Have some sexy lingerie at hand. Your partner will very much appreciate your attention to detail.

Most of all for your bedroom, create a warm, sensual space where you will feel free to relax and let go of any worry or anxiety for a few hours.

Guidelines for Success

Finally, I suggest a few guidelines to help maximize your enjoyment of your date night at home together.

First, I recommend you take steps to address any sexual response issues that may affect your ability to take pleasure in having sex together. These include erectile dysfunction (ED) and premature ejaculation (PE) for men, and pain with intercourse and vaginismus for women. Each of these conditions, and your feelings about them, can be exacerbated by anxiety. They can make for especially frustrating experiences with sex during the high-stress time of the coronavirus pandemic, but there are some things you can do to tackle them.

In each case, the first step is to have a consultation and examination with a physician, typically a urologist for men or a gynecologist for women. It might also be helpful to visit a practitioner, such as a naturopathic doctor, who specializes in sexual medicine. You want to learn whether or not you have any underlying medical conditions that may be affecting your performance, and if so, how to get treatment.

For men with ED, the next step is to experiment with changing your behavior in ways that might help. ED can often be treated with medications that facilitate erections, such as Viagra or Cialis. If this approach does not work for you, find a qualified sex therapist, get help from some of the resources in Chapter 8 that deal with men's sexuality (such as *Great Sex* by Michael Castleman), or follow the suggestions in this next scenario.

A common situation I encounter in my practice is a man who has erection difficulties when having sex with his partner, but has little or no problem when masturbating alone, often with porn. This would indicate that the ED likely has psychological or behavioral roots. What I recommend here is to first go on a "porn fast." Just put it aside for perhaps a few weeks to give your system a chance to reset. In the meantime, talk with your partner about how you can change your style of lovemaking to reduce the pressure to perform. Take orgasm (for yourself) off the table temporarily. Experiment with the Full Body Caressing exercises in Chapter 4. Ask your partner to give you more oral or manual stimulation of your penis. Slow down, savor the sensual pleasure in the moment, and enjoy the journey without any focus on your own orgasm as the destination. This approach has been helpful for many couples I have worked with.

In the same vein, Michael Castleman and others spell out the details of various self-treatment strategies for PE. These strategies mostly involve learning more about your arousal patterns and then adjusting your techniques—both alone and with your partner—to gain more ejaculatory control. Rather than thinking about baseball (or some other distraction), try to be aware of the sensations inside your penis so that you can better control your ejaculation. With masturbation, this can involve stop-start touching, and with partner sex, slow vaginal insertion and changing intercourse positions.

What's most important is to learn to identify your point of orgasmic inevitability—the point beyond which you simply *must* ejaculate. Practice bringing yourself close to that point— say, 80%—then backing off a bit, either by slowing down or stopping and taking a few deep breaths. Then slowly and gently work your way back toward that point again. Repeat these steps as often as needed. With a little practice, you should be able to train yourself to last much longer.

For women, vaginal dryness can be a source of irritation or pain during penis-in-vagina (PIV) sex. Again, get a medical exam to rule out any physical causes. Make sure your provider does a blood test to measure your levels of sex hormones, including estrogen, progesterone, and testosterone. (Yes, women have testosterone, too!) Your physician may recommend medications or supplements to boost your hormone levels, which decline naturally as you move through menopause. Also, use plenty of sexual lubricant ("lube") to ease penetration. Experiment with different lubes (I recommend water-based products) to see what works best. The key is to go slowly: start with fingers, then perhaps a dildo, and gradually move on to PIV sex when you're ready.

A related issue for women is vaginismus, a less-common condition in which the vaginal muscles have contracted so tightly that penetration is not physically possible. This condition can be successfully treated with pelvic floor therapy, typically administered over a period of time by a specially-trained physical therapist. By physically massaging and manipulating the muscles around the vagina and nearby areas, a pelvic floor therapist can help open things up so that penetration becomes possible again.

Here are some other guidelines that address issues around alcohol, privacy, and preparing for your date night. If you do consume alcohol, do so only in moderation. Having one or two drinks can enhance your mood for romance and sex. But too much might cause performance issues for men, inhibited orgasms for women, or drowsiness for either of you. Be mindful about your alcohol use and don't spoil your date night by becoming too intoxicated.

Make this your special time alone together. If you have other family members in the house, tell them that you need some private time without interruptions. If you have young children at home, you may need to schedule your date night for later in the evening after the kids have gone to bed. If you don't have one already, install a privacy lock on your bedroom door. Turn off your phones or leave them in another room. Try to take care of any potential demands ahead of time. The goal is for you and your lover to be fully present in the moment and engaged with each other.

Savor the anticipation and leverage it with your partner. As you go through the day leading up to your date night, pay extra attention to your mate. Be helpful around the house or apartment. Put some simple love notes in unexpected places for a pleasant surprise. Give a back rub and whisper naughty suggestions about the evening ahead.

It's important to keep your relationship vital and energized as much as you can during the time you are quarantined together. Planning some date nights at home is an excellent way to connect in a deeper and meaningful way. And you'll enjoy some sexual pleasure, too!

Chapter 3
Be Mindful about Sex

The present moment is filled with joy and happiness.
If you are attentive, you will see it.

THÍCH NHẤT HẠNH

C hances are you've heard about mindfulness. It's a deceptively simple, yet very effective technique for gaining a certain type of self-mastery. Millions of people have learned the basics of mindfulness meditation in recent decades. Perhaps you even use it to reduce stress and relieve anxiety in your everyday life.

Mindfulness is the practice of paying attention to what is happening in the moment, without any thoughts about the past or the future.

Here's how it works. At any time in your waking hours you can decide to enter a mindful state. When you do, you'll pause for a moment and pay attention to your breath. Notice how you're breathing. Then notice any other feelings in your body—muscle aches, joint pains, pleasurable contentment—whatever is there at that moment. Then, become directly aware of what you are doing and what is happening in your environment.

It's simple, but it's not that easy. What *is* easy is for your mind to wander. You lose touch with your body and start fixating again on unhelpful thoughts: recent events, plans for your next activity, general worries. You return to your "monkey mind" and go chasing one thought to the next, losing your presence in the moment.

Once you realize that you've wandered, simply remind yourself to return to your center. Notice your breath again and regain awareness of your body and your environment. Many people report that mindfulness is like having an internal "witness" who simply observes and notes what's happening without judgment.

Good things usually happen when you access a mindful state. You slow down and relax. You may sense a certain calmness coming over you. You have more patience, both with yourself and with others. You become less reactive. You are better able to redirect your impulses, analyze a situation, and make reasoned choices.

The pioneering work over the last thirty years by Jon Kabat-Zinn, PhD, has brought mindfulness meditation into both mainstream culture and clinical research. Numerous studies have documented that mindfulness can alleviate stress and anxiety, reduce pain, strengthen the immune system, improve sleep quality, and much more.

Mindfulness and Sex

What does this have to do with sex? Entering a mindful state during lovemaking can help you be more present in the moment so you can fully surrender to sexual ecstasy. It helps you get out of your head and into your body. This tool is a powerful mind-body connector that you can leverage for heightened sexual pleasure.

Many of my clients report that their minds wander during sex. This was a problem for Shirley and Jason, who had been together for about eight years. They both had plenty of desire for each other, and acted on it frequently, but the sex had become boring. It just felt routine, like they were stuck in a rut. They wanted my help to reignite their passion for each other.

Shirley had started a new job that she loved, and she found that once lovemaking got underway, her thoughts would drift to some pressing work issue. This interfered with her enjoyment of sex. Jason, who was now working remotely from home, had a similar problem regarding all the household duties that fell to him. He would be in the middle of pleasurable sex when he would suddenly remember a chore that needed to get done. Each partner's mental distraction would break the erotic spell between them. They were both very motivated to find a solution.

My suggestion to each of them was this: when you notice that your attention has wandered, tell your partner, and then pause what you're doing. Take several deep breaths, and then resume your sexual interaction, but now describe in detail—out loud—exactly what is happening. For example, Jason could say, "I am continuing to thrust my cock into your pussy. I can see it going in and out. It feels good." Or Shirley could say, "I am enjoying the sensations of your mouth on my pussy. I love it when you nibble on my labia." The more detail, the better. Keep the descriptions going for a few moments until you feel yourself refocusing on the sexual experience.

This may seem pretty simple, but it takes some work. At first, Shirley and Jason were embarrassed to disclose that their minds had wandered. They each felt that this was some sort of admission of failure or that it reflected badly on their desire for each other.

After some reassurance that this was a normal phenomenon, they agreed to practice giving the detailed descriptions in the moment. This was especially awkward for Shirley because she found it difficult to talk about sex. I encouraged her to try some of the exercises I mention in Chapter 1 ("Talking about Sex"), and those seemed to help. Eventually they both became more comfortable with this technique and found that it brought them back to the present moment more easily. Jason remarked, "I used to think that talking about sex during sex would be a turnoff. But it's just the opposite. Now it gets us hotter and our minds don't wander nearly as much!"

This mind-wandering during sex happens with most people at some point. Psychologists call it "spectatoring." When you drift off to other thoughts while making love, you weaken your connection with your body and its sensations. And that can derail your pleasure (and your partner's pleasure, too).

The two most common forms of spectatoring during sex are worrying about how your body looks and worrying about how you are performing sexually. Women tend to focus more on the body image issues, men more on the performance concerns. It's hard to be fully present when you are thinking of one thing while doing another.

So how do you practice mindfulness during sex? The trick is to *remember*. This will be easier if you start by practicing with everyday activities. You can apply mindfulness to almost anything you do.

A typical example would be brushing your teeth. Instead of letting your mind wander while you perform this familiar and repetitive task, spend those two minutes paying attention to the details of what you're doing. Sense the pressure of the brush on your teeth and gums. Taste the toothpaste. Look in the mirror to observe how you're holding the toothbrush. Feel the toothpaste and saliva accumulate in your mouth. If you notice your mind drifting off to extraneous thoughts, just return to your center and resume your mindful observations.

Mindfulness Exercise

You can practice mindfulness during an endless variety of activities, such as taking a walk, folding laundry, or sweeping the floor. Here I suggest that you take a mindful approach to something that you are perhaps doing more often now: *washing your hands.*

Hand washing has suddenly become much more meaningful as an effective way to diminish the spread of the coronavirus (and other germs, too). The need for regular hand washing—especially after contact with anyone or anything outside your home—is critical. If you're serious about avoiding infection, then I'm willing to bet that hand washing now has a lot more of your attention and that you are remembering to do it as needed.

Here are the steps for practicing mindfulness while washing your hands:

1. When you return from an errand or from having outside contact, focus on the *need* to wash your hands.

2. As you move toward the bathroom or kitchen to begin, *remember* that you are going to be mindful.

3. Turn on the water and soap up your hands.

4. Notice the temperature of the water and how the soap feels on your hands.

5. Pay attention to thoroughly washing every part of your hands: the backs and palms, the thumbs and wrists, between the fingers, and the fingernails.

6. Continue for at least 20 seconds (the recommended time for a complete cleaning).

7. As you rinse and dry your hands, notice the feeling of the towel on your skin and how your skin goes from wet to dry.

8. Hang up the towel and congratulate yourself on two accounts: First, you washed your hands! Second, you were mindful of the process!

Take a couple of deep breaths and notice how a mindful experience of washing your hands imparts a higher sense of presence and awareness.

Paying Attention during Sex

Once you become more comfortable with a little mindfulness here and there throughout the day, it could be time to apply this to some bedroom activity. One tactic is to establish a specific activity in advance as a cue or trigger for you to remember to be mindful. For example, you might say to yourself, "The first time I touch my partner's genitals, I will pause and be mindful about the moment. I will pay close attention to how it feels and how my partner is responding." Notice if your thoughts wander, then merely let them go and return to your center.

I am not suggesting that you spend your entire time having sex in a state of mindfulness (although it is possible). Instead, use this technique at a few points along the way to pause and check in with yourself and your partner.

Here are some things that you can observe in a mindful moment during sex:

- **Inner State.** What are your thoughts, feelings, and intentions for this lovemaking session? How do you feel about your partner?

- **Sensory Experience.** What sounds do you notice: loud or soft music, moaning or groaning by either of you? What do you see: your partner's face and body, parts of your own body? Where is your skin touching your partner and your surroundings? Are you aware of any smells or tastes?

- **Verbal expressions.** Are you or your partner expressing pleasure verbally, saying what you like (or don't like)? Notice the silences, too.

- **Physical actions.** What movements, positions, touching, and nonverbal communication are you and your partner engaged in? How is your breathing? Slow and easy, or fast and energetic?

- **Physiological responses.** What do you notice in your body or your partner's body? Are there signs of arousal and excitement such as warmth and tingling, particularly in the genital area?

This is a lot to pay attention to, and I'm not saying that you should run through these suggestions like a checklist. Rather, use your mindful moment to tune into one or two specific observations that catch your attention, especially pleasurable sensations. You may even want to tell your partner what you are noticing during a moment of mindfulness.

These moments can help you tune in more closely to sexual signals, both from your partner and from your own body. They help you tune out distracting thoughts or concerns. They help you make better choices about what to do or how to respond as you continue making love. And that can lead to more arousal, pleasure, and satisfaction for both of you.

Remember: when your mind wanders, just notice the errant thoughts. Then pause, take a deep breath, and return to your mindful moment.

Loving Kindness

Mindfulness can stimulate increased awareness and calm, and a sense that, despite your current challenges, everything will be OK. It can give you an expansive and inclusive perspective on reality. It can open your heart to feelings of love and thoughts of kindness toward others. There are even specific "loving kindness" meditations or guided imagery to help cultivate this quality.

What I would like to encourage you to do is to direct some of that loving kindness toward *yourself*—especially in that moment when you're having sex and some of those distracting thoughts begin to intrude on your erotic interlude.

You may start to imagine that your body is not good enough or that your partner is judging your appearance or behavior. Or you may start to worry about whether or not your sexual performance will please your partner. Perhaps your mind wanders to the to-do list, or you start to ruminate on the global pandemic. In those flashes of disconnection from yourself, remember to stop, take a deep breath, and return to the present moment.

Your concerns may have some validity, and you can use them as motivation to make some changes over time. But in that sensual moment, please be kind to yourself. Remind yourself to be more accepting of who you are and where you are in that very moment. Be grateful for all that you have. Take a deep breath and return to your lovemaking with a renewed sense of acceptance of yourself and your partner.

One final note. I have mentioned the breath throughout this chapter because it can be a powerful key to unlock these deeper states of consciousness. But there's also a hidden sexual benefit to mindful breathing. The more deep breaths you take, the more you oxygenate your blood, and—guess what—research shows that deep breathing can promote more frequent and more intense orgasms. How about that for a double benefit!

Chapter 4
Use Touch to Relieve Stress

Most men pursue pleasure with such breathless haste that they hurry past it.

SØREN KIERKEGAARD

Now, more than ever, we need comforting touch: a touch of love. Our sense of touch is critical to our survival. In childhood, when early experiences of touch are ideally abundant and loving, we learn to associate touch with trust, safety, warmth, closeness, and serenity. Body-to-body contact nurtures our inner child throughout our lifetime. It is the most basic and profound language for communicating comfort, care, affection, pleasure, and passion.

Receiving touch (and giving it, too) provides a number of physical and mental health benefits. Touch can soothe muscle tension and reduce stress. Touch releases the "cuddle hormone" oxytocin, which enhances your sense of trust and attachment, and induces feelings of calmness, pleasantness, and mild euphoria. Touch can even boost the immune system and lower blood pressure.

Of course, touching and intimacy go hand in hand. Connecting skin-to-skin is a fundamental component of enjoying satisfying sexual relations.

With all these benefits, you might expect that couples in quarantine would be affectionately touching each other more often. But living in close quarters 24 hours a day, with minimal breaks from each other, can become emotionally and physically overwhelming. As the stay-at-home restrictions wear on week by week, touching—or being touched—might become downright irritating.

This is all the more reason to develop a conscious approach to touch so that you can maintain your sanity while enjoying the comfort and stimulation of warm and caring physical contact.

What is a conscious approach to touch? In essence, it means making some agreements with your partner about how the two of you will touch each other. I recommend that you try the strategy laid out in the Guidelines for Daily Touch section below. Agree together to set boundaries, give feedback, and express affection. This will allow you to manage your expectations of each other in healthy ways as you go about your day at home together. Equally important, agree with your partner to set aside specific times to engage in intentional, sensual exploration together. This exploration is not necessarily meant to result in sex, but to be pursued for the pure pleasure and benefits of loving touch.

Guidelines for Daily Touch

How you touch your partner (and how your partner touches you) can sometimes be tricky to navigate, even under the best of circumstances. But when you are "locked down" together, as during the COVID-19 pandemic, the stakes can be higher because of the increased stress and anxiety inherent in the situation.

I recently had some online sessions with a couple who were in a rut regarding their negative touch patterns: Bill and Susan, married, in their early 50s, whose children were grown and established out of the home. They wanted their empty nest to become a love nest. Susan told me, "I want to feel desire again." Bill wanted more touch and physical connection with his wife. He needed physicality in order to show his tenderness and his longing to connect with her. Bill complained sadly, "I can't seem to find the words. Intimacy talk eludes me." Susan was more verbally oriented and felt that words were safer than gestures and movements.

Both of them were worried that their patterns of touching (and not touching) would become exacerbated by having to spend a lot more time together during the lockdown. When Bill would try to express his affection for Susan by giving her a hug or rubbing her neck and shoulders, Susan would grudgingly accept his touch. But after only a brief moment of touching, Susan would pull away or deflect further physical contact. Susan felt that his approaches were disguised invitations to be sexual, and she was not ready for that. She wanted to feel some desire first before she assented to be sexual. As a result, Bill would feel rejected and Susan would feel more detached from any potential passion in her body.

So, we created a simple plan. I coached Bill on how to approach Susan in a more conscious and intentional way. For example, before he touched Susan, he would tell her that he wanted to give her a hug, and say whether or not it was intended to have any sexual overtones. Susan was then free to say yes or no to the hug.

With a little practice, they learned how to incorporate this strategy into their daily routines. This helped Bill begin learning to voice his feelings; it also helped Susan feel more in control of her body. She reported that when Bill would tell her there were no sexual motives involved in a hug, she could relax and enjoy the contact much more, trusting that she wasn't expected to become aroused. And when Bill did announce a sexual intention, Susan felt free to make a choice rather than accept the hug out of obligation. They gradually started touching each other more, which unlocked the healing benefits of touch for them and their relationship.

You can adopt this kind of strategy for yourselves by following these guidelines:

- **Respect Boundaries.** Have a talk where each of you clarifies how you like to touch and be touched during the day. Do the same for what kind of touching you don't like. Be specific and make sure that each of you understands the other. Then, as you go forward, respect each other's boundaries. (Note: the Body Survey exercise below can help with this discussion.)

- **Give Feedback.** If the touch feels good, say so. (Sighs of approval and soft moans also work!) If the touch is not so good, say so...and if possible, say what *would* feel good so your partner can adjust. Also, speak up if you feel your boundaries have been compromised.

- **Express Affection.** Talk while you're touching and tell your partner something loving or appreciative. Use your words to reinforce the healing power of your touch. Remember, it's OK to ask to be touched. Who can resist their lover's heartfelt request of: "I need a hug?"

- **Schedule Time for Sensual Touch.** I encourage you: Don't neglect this guideline. The first three guidelines are more like survival strategies, and I hope they help your relationship while sheltering at home.

This fourth guideline is your ticket to pleasurable adventures with your partner even in non-pandemic times. You'll find details for several sensual touch exercises below. Pick the ones you like and put them on your calendar!

These guidelines are intended to help each of you maintain distance when needed and embrace intimacy when desired. Of course, in moments of spontaneous playfulness or consensual passion, the boundaries may come down. No problem. But for maintaining daily sanity, the guidelines can be very helpful.

As soon as you schedule a sensual touch exercise, you are likely to have some feelings in anticipation of this session with your partner. Perhaps you feel some excitement about the prospect of tactile pleasure. Or perhaps you feel some fear or trepidation.

Touch is a very powerful force strongly connected to our emotions. If you have experienced trauma or neglect in your past, you may not be so keen on the idea of intentional sensual touching. That's OK. It's important to identify where you find yourself on the diverse human spectrum of tactile affinity, between touchy-feely at one end and touch-averse at the other. If an exercise seems scary, be creative and adjust the parameters so that it becomes a baby step for you. Every movement toward change begins this way. Take advantage of your time together to be a little adventurous.

Imagine yourself approaching these exercises with a spirit of curiosity, with an openness to the possibility that you might learn something. You're likely feeling some anticipation about this new experience. That anticipation is programmed to give you a bonus: dopamine! It's the neurotransmitter associated with pleasure and reward. Simply put, it feels good. Studies show that dopamine is released in large amounts when we anticipate a pleasurable experience. Use this information to your own advantage.

Sensual Touch Exercises

These exercises are designed to help you and your partner get more comfortable with touching and being touched. By touching more, you can start to break out of any negative tactile patterns you might be stuck in. Instead, you can learn to harness the healing power of touch to improve your well-being and counteract the stresses of daily life, especially while in quarantine.

Your body is your natural partner in this process. As you start to shift more toward conscious and sensual touching, the release of oxytocin creates a positive feedback loop that floods you with good feelings. The more we experience healing touch, the more we want to be touched. It's pleasurable, and when we feel pleasure, it's hard to feel sad, anxious, or stressed. I hope you find pleasurable rewards in this journey with your partner.

The first exercise (The Body Survey) is fairly nonthreatening for anyone who may be more touch averse, and you only need to do it once. In fact, it doesn't even involve any actual touching. The second exercise (The 7-Second Kiss and the 15-Second Hug) is something you can do in less than one minute every day. The third exercise (Being Held) is great for helping relieve stress and anxiety at any time. Just remember that these first three exercises are not necessarily meant to lead directly to sexual activity.

The final exercise (Full-Body Caressing) is a progressive series of increasingly intimate touching. Use this exercise to go deeper as you discover that there is much more to physical sexual intimacy than a narrow focus on genitals.

48

Body Survey Exercise

The purpose of this exercise is to check in with each other about where on your body you like to be touched and where you don't. First, draw a rough outline of a body (torso, head, limbs) on a piece of paper, similar to a paper doll cutout. Then use green and red markers to mark on the outline those places where you like to be touched (green) and those places where you don't want to be touched (red). Use word labels as needed for clarification.

When each of you has finished marking your outlines, compare with your partner and discuss the details. This is an easy way for you and your partner to practice clear communication about touching. You just might learn something new! It's also a great adjunct to the "Respect Boundaries" guideline above.

The 7-Second Kiss and the 15-Second Hug

When you give your partner a quick kiss and hug, as people often do upon leaving or returning home, it helps to maintain the bond between you. It's a short ritual that says: "I love you and value you."

Some couples, however, particularly those who have been together a number of years, tend to fall out of the habit of using touch to express affection for each other. Days and days can pass without a kiss or hug. This exercise, which can be fun and enjoyable, is the perfect antidote.

The exercise is nothing more than extending the time you kiss and hug your partner. Why? Because studies have shown that seven seconds is the minimum length of time it takes for kissing to stimulate the release of the hormone oxytocin. Hugging takes a little longer. The idea is to prolong your kiss and hug so that both of you can experience warm feelings of well-being—the benefits of an extra shot of oxytocin.

How do you incorporate this activity (which I like to call my 7/15 exercise) into your daily routine? The challenge is to remember to do it. Establishing a trigger event can be a helpful reminder. Perhaps you agree to a 7/15 hug and kiss right before dinner every evening. Or maybe you do this right before you share coffee or tea in the morning. It doesn't matter when, just that you remember and follow through every day.

Here's an idea: since the exercise is called 7/15, you could plan to have a prolonged hug and kiss at or around 7:15 a.m. (if you get up that early!). Or maybe you designate 7:15 p.m. as the trigger time. Use whatever works to help you remember to connect in this way. If you have small children around your home, don't be surprised if they want to join in, making it a family hug. Kids can sense the good feelings generated by a 7/15 hug and kiss.

Being Held Exercise

In my thirty-plus years of working with couples, I have found that sex is only a part of adult intimacy. We all need to be held, to be emotionally connected; seeing and holding each other helps provide safety and security. Some people use sex as a way to create a substitute for the sense of connection they need. I would guess that many men or women have engaged in sex just to meet their need for being held.

This exercise provides the benefits of emotional connection without the need to be sexual. It is a straightforward, nonsexual activity. It might be something that you are already doing together. The idea here is to be intentional about it. You can do this standing up, sitting on a couch, lying in bed, or any other position that works for you. Just remember, this is not an invitation to have sex. If you like, agree in advance about the amount of time you want to devote to this exercise (perhaps five or ten minutes).

One partner says to the other: "I would like to be held" (or you can offer by asking: "Would you like me to hold you?") Then take a few minutes where one of you simply holds the other person in their arms. I recommend that neither partner talks during this time, except to briefly negotiate a more comfortable position if needed.

For the person being held, take some deep breaths and relax into the moment. Allow yourself to be surrounded by the safety and comfort of your partner. You may even imagine yourself as a small child. Feel the security of your attachment to your partner. It's OK to cry. Just try to refrain from talking while you are being held.

For the person doing the holding, your role is to act as a silent support. Simply hold your partner and "be there" for them. Don't stroke or try to comfort your partner. Just be a loving and accepting presence, allowing the moment to unfold with no goal in mind.

Then disengage, switch roles, and repeat the process. If you were the holder in the first part of the exercise, you might not be feeling the need to be held. But do it anyway. It helps balance the energies between you.

When you both feel complete, take a few minutes to discuss what came up for each of you, both as the holder and the one being held. It's important to listen carefully and acknowledge each other's feelings. (The Deep Listening exercise from Chapter 1 can help with this kind of tender communication.) You might be surprised to discover that sometimes the person doing the holding experiences the stronger emotional response.

Full-Body Caressing Exercise

Touch can be a gateway to more sexual connection. But intimate touch sometimes becomes a goal-focused sexual activity that is restricted to stimulation of the genital organs with the aim of producing orgasm. This narrow focus bypasses sensual touch and often leads to sexual difficulties such as performance anxiety, spectatoring, lack of arousal, and even boredom.

This four-stage set of exercises is based on the "sensate focus" protocols developed by pioneering sex researchers William Masters and Virginia Johnson in the 1960s. Millions of people continue to benefit from this approach to slowing down and engaging in more non-genital touching. It can help overcome sexual dysfunctions and can lead to increased sexual satisfaction.

The initial stages of the exercises are done without orgasm or intercourse. This strategy can alleviate the stress, pressure, and performance anxiety some couples may feel around intercourse. You can use these full-body caressing exercises with your partner to move beyond any negative or ambivalent attitudes toward partnered touch. Many clients have reported that these sensual touch exercises bring them to delightful new levels of sensual awareness and tactile pleasure.

Remember, these caressing exercises are not intended to elicit a sexual response in the initial stages; for example, breasts and genitalia are off-limits in the beginning. The sensual experience remains paramount. You explore each other's bodies through touching, stroking, and caressing in mutually gratifying ways. Use a light touch—this is caressing, not massage.

Set aside an agreed upon prearranged time, typically 60 minutes, where you will take turns being the Giver and the Receiver (30 minutes each). Be creative and enjoy each other, perhaps by taking a preparatory bubble bath or a shower together followed by a towel massage. Set the scene for a sensual encounter. Add soft music and romantic lighting, and turn up the heat so you'll be comfortable without your clothes on. Don't forget to silence or turn off electronic devices and lock the bedroom door if you need privacy.

Be self-aware and express your feelings through facial expression and sounds. I recommend you refrain from any verbal interaction during the exercises, except to report any discomfort when you are the Receiver. However, I encourage sighing and moaning as ways to give feedback to your partner in the moment.

The following activities may feel awkward at first. That's OK. Feel free to giggle! Trust that this progression will help lead you to sexual encounters that are more satisfying to you both. Try to enjoy yourself and remain open to your own and your partner's feelings and physical responses.

If at any point you experience anxiety or a negative feeling, stop. (Note to partner: don't take it personally. Reframe the break as a part of your learning journey together.) If possible, continue the connecting touch, perhaps with more gentle strokes, pausing to see if the anxiety subsides. If so, proceed with the exercise. If not, try again later.

How often should you do these exercises? I recommend that you practice at least one stage each week. You can, of course, repeat a stage, and you can also progress through the stages faster than once a week. Do what works for you.

Stage 1. Each partner takes a turn exploring the face, head, hands, and feet of the other partner. Touch first with your fingers or hand. Then you might progress to using your mouth or lips to caress. Use touches that vary in length, pressure, and intensity. Avoid the breasts and genitals. There is no intercourse or penetration in this stage. You can even do this stage fully clothed if you like. Or get naked—it's your choice. Remember, the initial goals are positive and connecting experiences, not arousal or orgasm.

Stage 2. Start with your clothes off and do the exercises from Stage 1. Then add light teasing by stroking the genitals and breasts. Take turns exploring your partner's entire body. There is still no intercourse at this stage. Avoid penetration or touching that leads to orgasm.

Stage 3. Begin with the pleasurable things you practiced in Stages 1 and 2, but now touch each other at the same time. Find ways of pleasuring each other simultaneously through touching, stroking, and kissing. Again, avoid any penetration or orgasm.

Stage 4. Take the time to go through the first three stages again. Slow things down and relax. Then move on to rubbing your bodies together for mutual pleasure. Feel free to engage in intercourse or orgasm. Or, if you're not ready, try several more sessions of this stage before you move on to penetration or orgasm. Anything goes for mutual satisfaction! Be creative and spend lots of time on full-body caressing.

Talk with each other after you complete each exercise. Between turns is a good time. Offer your partner feedback about how you felt emotionally and physically, both when you were the giver and the receiver of touch. Use specific adjectives rather than vague ones to describe your experience. For example, replace "great" or "wonderful" with descriptions like "flowing," "ticklish," "warm," "relaxing," "hard," "soothing," or "uncomfortable." You may want to write up some notes after the discussion to refer back to as you progress through the four stages.

Following these stages of the Full-Body Caressing exercise in sequence can help you discover the benefits of slowing down and paying more attention to your and your partner's total-body responses. As you learn to ease into lovemaking, you'll find that prolonging the slow pleasure of sensual body intimacy will intensify your ultimate levels of arousal and satisfaction.

Tips for Massage

Of course, a massage from a loved one can feel really good. It's a great stress reliever and it helps ease aches and pains. Studies have shown that the person giving the massage gets as much benefit as the person receiving the touch (another opportunity for a positive feedback loop).

You can approach your partner to give or receive a massage using any of the interactions described in the exercises above. The process should be smooth if you both are clear about your intentions, communicate directly, express your feelings, give each other feedback, and respect boundaries. Try not to take a refusal personally; just schedule another time, if you can. Taking turns massaging each other is a good way to help keep your relationship in balance.

Be creative in your approach to couples' massage. There is such a range of options:

- Give a two-minute back rub or devote an hour to a full body massage.

- Use lotion or oil for lubrication. Or nothing at all.

- Schedule a session in advance or be spontaneous.

- Impromptu neck and shoulder rubs are especially good at relieving stress.

- Use different parts of your hands: your fingers, your palm, the side of your hand.

- Vary the pressure of your touch.

- Foot rubs can be soothing or exciting.

- As the giver, check in to find out how your partner is doing.

- As the receiver, give frequent feedback about what feels good or not so good.

- Uncertain about your massage skills? Watch some tutorials on YouTube.

A final note: Consider the possibility of massaging and sexually stimulating your partner *at the same time.* Your first thought might be, "How can you do both at once? Wouldn't one distract from the other?" Without some forethought this mashup might seem counterproductive. But if you take your time to play with various techniques, you may find something that works well for you. This combination—a healing sexual massage—does take creativity and practice, but the benefits can be astounding.

For example, start by massaging your partner's thigh muscles with one hand and using your other hand for genital stroking. The key here is to find the right balance between the two, and verbal feedback from your partner is essential. Too much emphasis on the genitals and your partner may not benefit much from the massage strokes. Too much emphasis on the massage and your partner may not notice any enhancement from the sexual arousal.

Experiment with various body parts, types of sexual stimulation, and body positions (for each of you). It might help if you visualize the flow of sexual energy through the body, moving back and forth between the muscles being massaged and the genital area. Also visualize the flow between the two of you. Pay special attention to synchronizing your massage and genital strokes with any rhythmic pelvic movements you detect in your partner. Music with the right tempo can enhance the experience.

Once you get the hang of it, combining massage and sexual stimulation can have powerful healing results. Sore muscles get an extra shot of feel-good hormones produced by sexual arousal. In turn, sexual arousal is boosted by the muscles' release of stress. Pleasure and healing abound. This is another one of those positive feedback loops that you can nurture and expand with practice. And it's a heck of a lot of fun!

The healing power of touch is literally right at your fingertips. I hope you'll use it wisely to deepen your experience of pleasure and discover new realms of intimacy with your partner.

Chapter 5
Revitalize Your Senses

The five senses are the ministers of the soul.

LEONARDO DA VINCI

B eing stuck at home during a pandemic can have some advantages. You can skip taking a shower if you want. You can nap when you feel like it. You can lounge around in your pajamas all day. (I saw a recent internet meme that read: "8 p.m. is now the official time to change from your day pajamas into your evening pajamas.")

Confinement in the same environment for weeks on end also has many downsides, some of which are serious matters. Here's one that may have escaped your attention: *sensory monotony.* This is a gradual dulling of the senses that can lead to boredom, cognitive decline, stress, and mental health problems. NASA has studied this phenomenon in its efforts to find effective ways to maintain robust sensory engagement for astronauts traveling on long journeys through space. Indeed, living through a global pandemic can make you feel like you're on an interminable spaceflight to nowhere.

Our five primary senses—vision, hearing, touch, taste, and smell—can all become blunted by monotony. But they aren't the only ones. We have a sense of balance. We are able to sense hot and cold. We can sense where our bodies are in the space around us (known as proprioception). In fact, some scientists claim we have as many as twenty different sensory modalities.

But our senses can get lazy. Being in quarantine makes it even easier to zone out in front of the TV, incessantly browse social media sites, or search for "just one more" video to entertain you. The problem is that despite the small hits of dopamine you get from each new and different distraction, your body and your senses eventually become lethargic and dull. Your muscles lose tone. Colors appear muted. The normally pleasant sounds of music and voices seem unexciting or possibly irritating. Tastes and smells—even from your favorite foods—lose some appeal. This is not good for your mental health, and it certainly is not good for your sex life.

Maintain Sensory Engagement

To counteract these effects, I encourage you to adopt some practices that will keep your body and your senses feeling more engaged and alive. Much of this is common sense, but I want to offer a few suggestions that will help you stay sharp:

- **Limit your screen viewing.** Staring at phones, tablets, desktops, or televisions can eat up your time and deaden your emotional affect. Set a timer or other controls to help you remember to take a screen break or to turn your devices off for the evening.

- **Get outdoors often.** It's especially important to go out in nature if possible. Take a walk. Hold hands with your partner as you stroll around your neighborhood. Do some gardening or yardwork if you can. Go for a run or a bike ride. Of course, make sure you follow any social distancing guidelines in effect.

- **Learn a new skill.** You likely have more free time on your hands while in quarantine. Use this opportunity in productive and creative ways to expand your talents. Learn to juggle. Play an instrument. Acquire a new language. Perform a magic trick. The learning process gets both your body and your mind involved in creating new sensory and motor nerve connections that improve your cognitive functioning.

- **Regulate your consumption of news.** Yes, it's important to stay informed about daily events involving the pandemic. But information overload, especially the doom-and-gloom variety so prevalent these days, creates anxiety and can distort your perception of reality. I suggest you set aside a certain time each day (no more than an hour) during which you choose to read or view news. Then free up the rest of your day for more constructive activities or just to relax.

Strategies like these—and many others as well—are designed to help you cope with the stresses brought on by this pandemic. Being proactive about your own physical and mental health will help you ride the waves of this social upheaval.

Sensual Pleasures

Maintaining your physical and mental health will also help you enjoy sensual pleasures. In turn, experiencing pleasure promotes your health and happiness. It's another positive feedback loop.

The varieties of sensual pleasures are endless. In the remainder of this section, I suggest fun ways to indulge different senses in four types of pleasurable activities: food, music, body pampering, and kissing. I encourage you to do these with your partner so that you both keep sharp.

Food

The process of cooking and eating engages most of your senses. You get loads of touch stimulation from doing hands-on preparation—peeling, chopping, combining ingredients, sautéing, etc. You can engage your visual awareness with an appealing presentation of your culinary creations. Of course, the experience of eating brings delightful tastes and smells, and you engage your sense of touch as you chew and swallow, especially if you slow down and savor the experience.

The renewed popularity of baking at home during the pandemic supports the value of these sensual delights. If cooking gets monotonous or tedious, order some takeout to sample different tastes and cuisines. You can even meet with friends for a virtual dinner party on a videoconferencing application such as Zoom. Having some novelty in your dining experiences will help you offset boredom and fatigue.

Preparing and eating food at home with your partner can become a sensual prelude to sex. Make "gastronomic foreplay" a part of your date night at home. Here are a few suggestions to spice things up:

- **Dress up for dinner at home.** Sure, you can wear jeans and a t-shirt when you grab a quick bite for supper at the kitchen table. But how about occasionally dressing up as if you were going out for dinner as a couple? Create a special meal together. Set the table with cloth napkins and candlelight to add a touch of class. It's a great little escape from your daily routine.

- **Feed each other hand-to-mouth.** This often works best with dessert. Some of my sensual favorites include chocolate covered strawberries, grapes (fresh or frozen), watermelon slices, and chocolate truffles. To maximize your enjoyment, take turns feeding each other *very slowly*. Don't rush through it. Take the time to delight in feeding your partner and to savor the taste and texture of the food.

- **Try aphrodisiac foods.** Although there is little scientific evidence that any foods actually cause a measurable increase in libido, you might want to try some just for fun. Folklore from many cultures is replete with suggestions, including watermelon, chocolate, oysters, asparagus, chili peppers, figs, strawberries, and many more. Get some great recipes from the book *Simple Sexy Food* by Linda De Villers, PhD, which I describe in the Books section of Chapter 8.

- **Have a *Tom Jones*-style feast.** Winner of the Oscar for Best Picture in 1963, *Tom Jones* is a British comedy that includes a classic scene in the history of film cuisine. Actors Albert Finney and Joyce Redman voraciously consume a huge meal at a country inn, each gorging on the food with their hands and fingers in increasingly animalistic style. And they do this while looking lustily at each other and without speaking a word, letting their arousal build before they run off (presumably) to bed together. It's a memorable sensual experience on the screen; imagine how you could recreate your own slurpy, sloppy feast at home.

Music

"If music be the food of love, play on," wrote William Shakespeare in the first line of *Twelfth Night*. He knew about the powerful sensual effect that music can have on people, especially on their romantic inclinations. As you continue to endure your day-in, day-out existence at home, listening to music can provide stimulation in different ways. It can be soothing or energizing. It can be uplifting or melancholic. It can move your body or put you to sleep. It can turn you off or turn you on. Like the soundtrack to a movie, the music you choose to fill your space throughout the day can be a powerful tool to set the scene for any mood you wish to create.

Here are several types of music that I recommend you and your partner might like to share:

- **Favorite songs.** Think back to the music that you enjoyed listening to around the time you and your partner first met. Did the two of you have any songs you both liked? What about music that has played a part in your courtship and continued relationship? My husband and I have several songs that hold special meaning for us. A favorite is "Beyond the Sea" by Bobby Darin. (The closing line of the song— *"And never again I'll go sailing"*—signifies for us that the search is over. We found each other!) Dig out your favorites and listen to them together. Let the music bring back some of the feelings you have experienced in special moments with your partner.

- **Dance music.** I offer some dance suggestions in the next chapter, Laugh and Play Together (including doing a striptease). I heartily recommend dancing as a way to open up your senses, including your sense of rhythm. It's good exercise and provides opportunities to bond with your partner.

- **Romantic melodies.** Love songs and sentimental ballads can create a very romantic mood. Even if you or your partner are not interested in the stories told by the songs, the tempo and arrangements can slow things down and help you relax into the moment. This mood can help you ease into some foreplay. But if you want things to heat up, you might benefit from something more energetic.

- **Fuck music.** Plain and simple, this is loud music with a strong, driving beat that roughly approximates the natural human rhythm of pelvic thrusting during sexual intercourse (about 100 beats per minute, or a little less than two beats per second). The idea is to let the music reinforce the vigor of your arousal. You'll find many classic rock songs, disco tracks, dance club favorites, as well as songs from other genres and many eras, in this category of music. Search online for suggestions to get you started, then create a playlist or station from those songs. On occasion, the right music with the right pulsation can significantly enhance the intensity of your orgasmic pleasure.

These are just a few of the ways that you can leverage music to help you find more pleasure in your days—and nights—together.

Body Pampering

Your body deserves to feel good. Decide on some bodily pleasures, apart from sex, that you enjoy. Then set aside the time to pamper yourselves and each other. In Chapter 4: Use Touch to Relieve Stress, I share a number of exercises that you and your partner could use to touch each other, as well as some tips on massage. Here are some more body-pampering activities for your indulgence:

- **Take a bath or shower together.** Let the hot water relax your muscles. Take in the fresh scents of soap and shampoo...or try a bubble bath! Wash your partner's body, including their genitals. Dry off your partner with freshly laundered towels. Feel all the good sensations of being in your body.

- **Rub each other down.** Use moisturizing lotion on your partner after your bath or shower together. Rub it in slowly to help relieve aches and pains. Enjoy the feeling of skin touching skin. This is a great time to express loving gratitude for each other as you allow healing touch to reinforce your feelings of love.

- **Try the champagne tingle.** In the bathtub together, take turns gently pouring a little champagne (freshly uncorked) on parts of your partner's body, such as arms or the chest. The tingling sensation on the skin from the sparkling bubbles is invigorating. Of course, you could drink some of the champagne, too. Finger foods would be another sensual addition.

Kissing

Kissing is a wonderful way to engage your senses, especially touch. Your lips and tongue are densely packed with nerve endings. They are loaded with sensors that give you pleasure when you kiss. Your sense of smell is also highly activated by the closeness of your face to your partner's body.

Kissing is one of the least threatening, and most exciting, ways to vary your intimacy. Try it soft or hard. Tongue or no tongue. Quick or prolonged. Dry or slurpy. Gentle or rough. And anywhere in between.

Many couples fall into a pattern where they stop kissing. Or they may give only a quick peck on the lips or cheek as a perfunctory ritual, without much sensory engagement. This is unfortunate because kissing has so much to offer. Check out the 7-Second Kiss and the 15-Second Hug exercise I describe in Chapter 4. This kind of intimacy leverages prolonged contact to stimulate the release of a whole raft of feel-good hormones and neurotransmitters. The health benefits of kissing include reduced stress and anxiety, and it can even lower your blood pressure.

To get back on track with your intimacy, experiment with your kissing repertoire! Take some time to explore together how each of you likes to kiss and be kissed. Maybe even try some new techniques to enhance your mutual pleasure. Here are some specific suggestions:

- **Reciprocal kissing**. You could start by kissing your partner the way you enjoy being kissed. Pause mid-kiss and say, "Mmmm, I love the way this feels." Then say, "Hey, would you show me what it feels like to be kissed by me just now?" By taking turns kissing, you each learn more about both the giving and receiving roles.

- **Soft kissing.** Surveys show that many women like to be kissed much more softly than the kisses they receive from their partners. Regardless of your partner's gender, take some time to slow down and relax as you ease into kissing. Start off gently. Kiss lightly and sensually around the mouth, the cheeks, or the back of the neck. When you reach your partner's mouth, kiss very softly on the lips without using your tongue. Going slowly is a sure way to build excitement.

- **Whole body kissing.** We usually imagine a kiss as a meeting of the mouths. But there are so many other areas of your partner's body to explore. In addition to the obvious targets (genitals and breasts), try different types of kisses on erogenous zones such as the neck, earlobe, armpit, wrist, feet, and toes. Not sure where to kiss? Just ask your partner.

For Jackie and Darnell, a young couple I counseled a few years ago, kissing turned out to be a revealing topic. They had been married for five years and Jackie felt like they were losing their connection, both physically and emotionally. Darnell had never been one to express much affection, but lately had gotten busier with his job and seemed to have less and less time to spend with his wife. The occasional sex was good, but often seemed obligatory and was mostly genitally focused. As Jackie said, "I feel like only part of Darnell is showing up in our relationship."

I first helped Jackie and Darnell work .on their communication skills and managing their expectations of each other. (Sometimes I have to do psychotherapy before I can do sex therapy.) They were both very motivated to keep their marriage intact. They practiced the Deep Listening exercise (mentioned in Chapter 1) and started to improve their connection. Jackie noticed that Darnell was being a little more attentive to her and would sometimes really listen rather than reacting defensively.

Next, they explored some touching exercises similar to those mentioned in Chapter 2 and made even further progress in reconnecting. But when I suggested they practice some of the kissing techniques described above, it really hit a nerve with Darnell. He basically refused to try them.

This became a sticking point between the two of them. Jackie, who really enjoyed the sensuality of her body, felt rejected. Darnell had some weak excuses about not wanting to try the kissing exercises, but they didn't hold up under scrutiny.

Finally, after some probing, Darnell recalled some incidents from his teenage years as he first started dating. When he would start to kiss a partner, he got so turned on that he would immediately put his tongue deep in her mouth. This was the "normal behavior" he saw modeled in movies and TV shows. But the young women he tried to aggressively French kiss would pull away from him. (Many women need to be substantially aroused before they enjoy deep, open-mouth kissing.)

This happened with several early partners, and over time he gradually learned to avoid kissing so he could avoid rejection.

Teasing out these memories proved to be a revelation for Darnell. He came to realize that he had put up emotional barriers to kissing as a way to avoid rejection, partly out of a subconscious fear of deeper intimacy with Jackie.

Darnell agreed to try the kissing exercises. After a few sessions, he was able to move beyond his initial discomfort and discovered that he actually liked kissing. The more they tried different ways of kissing, the more he liked it. And the more often they kissed, the more often they would enjoy hotter sex together.

Kissing is a powerful way to communicate. I encourage you to experiment with all the different possibilities for sensual pleasure that it can offer.

Confessions of a Sensualist

I believe in pleasure. I believe pleasure is a powerful force for healing and connection. I believe pleasure is everyone's birthright.

Pleasure can be a wonderful gateway to feeling more alive. Here's a quotation from my good friend and colleague Dr. Stella Resnick, taken from her book *The Pleasure Zone*:

How we enjoy ourselves affects our health. How well we can enjoy intimacy determines the depth and quality of our connection with others. How much pleasure we allow ourselves daily determines how fulfilled we are throughout our lifetimes.

Of course, there are other pleasures in addition to sensation. The mental pleasure of solving a problem or crafting a good sentence. The emotional pleasure of satisfying interactions with family and friends. The spiritual pleasure of knowing one's inner self and feeling a connection to one's higher purpose.

But as you may have surmised by now, I personally am most drawn to sensual pleasures, especially the sensuality of sex. Having good sex is such a grand, multisensory experience of intense pleasure, that I am compelled to seek more of it. I don't feel that anyone should be ashamed to claim this biological heritage.

As a sex therapist I practice what I preach. I want people to experience the pleasures and joys of good sex, and to experience the healing and happiness it can bring into your life. I am reminded of a quotation from lusty Mae West, a woman before her time: "Too much of a good thing can be wonderful!"

I hope you and your partner will partake in some of the sensual pleasures described in this chapter. Keeping your senses alive while enduring a monotonous quarantine will help you better manage your stress. Plus, you and your partner can have some fun together!

Chapter 6
Laugh and Play Together

Laughter is an instant vacation.

MILTON BERLE

Accroding to multiple studies, couples who laugh together last together. Research has shown that shared laughter (and even reminiscing about shared laughter from the past) has a positive effect on relationship satisfaction. Laughing and playing together strengthens the bond between couples. During my career I have helped many of my clients learn to put playfulness into their relationship—especially their sexual relationship. Yes, sex is play!

Nowhere are humor and fun more necessary than in the bedroom. Couples often experience tension and pressure surrounding their sex lives. Even under normal circumstances, a host of issues—differing expectations, miscommunication, mismatched levels of desire, and others—can make the marriage bed anything but a bed of roses. Add to that the stress and anxiety of life during a pandemic and it's no surprise that relationship problems are on the rise.

Creative silliness in life and in one's sex life may be the solution. After all, there is a three-year-old inside each one of us—a happy, giggling three-year-old. Let this child come out to play so that your relationship can be rejuvenated!

The Transactional Analysis model of human behavior, developed by Eric Berne and popularized by Thomas Harris in his book *I'm OK—You're OK*, is based on three ego-states: parent, adult, and child. The best sex occurs when each partner is acting from their "playful child" state. This is the part of oneself that knows how to live in the moment, conscious of no beginning, middle, or end.

One thing that gets in the way of play is the "critical parent." I have seen many clients who have difficulty letting themselves play at anything, much less sex. I often discover that they suffered heavy parental criticism growing up.

For many, learning to play as an adult is not easy. Years of negative conditioning leads to internalization of those disapproving messages. Play seems like a distant fantasy that only others can enjoy. Fortunately, laughter can lead the way back to play.

Laughter

Roger and Jenny, married 12 years, came to see me for help with their sex lives. Not long after their marriage, they lost the initial spark they had experienced during courtship. They loved each other, but the tensions around their infrequent sex bothered both of them. Jenny craved more excitement in their lovemaking. Roger was vaguely dissatisfied but couldn't say exactly why. He would often be disinterested in Jenny's tentative advances, which left her feeling frustrated.

Roger, it turned out, had a very demanding father whom he could never please. Even straight A's in school were not good enough! To compensate, Roger worked extremely hard and spent little time involved in leisure or recreational activities.

There was always a little more studying to do, and as an adult, a little more work to do for a deadline at his job.

My first task was to help Roger reconnect with laughter. It's not the same as play, but it's a big step in that direction. It turned out that he and Jenny used to like sketch comedy performances. So, my assignment to them was to watch some movies or shows like that together at home. And hopefully enjoy some laughs.

A good laugh, like a good cry or good sex, is a natural relaxant. Researchers have documented the physiological responses that happen when you laugh. A slight rise in heart rate and blood pressure accompany the laugh itself, and quickened breathing oxygenates the blood. But almost immediately after the laughing stops, the body muscles relax, and blood pressure drops. At the same time, the brain releases endorphins, nature's own opiates. These flood you with a mild sense of euphoria (or a massive sense of euphoria, as when you're rolling on the floor laughing!). It's no wonder we all love to laugh.

Roger and Jenny reported that they had fun watching some shows together. At one point Roger told Jenny that he felt like he was back in the time years ago when they first met. Although they cuddled a lot that evening, and Roger felt warm feelings for Jenny, he declined her invitation to have sex. I helped Roger dig a little deeper to see what held him back. He finally blurted out, "I just don't feel like I deserve to have that much fun."

This was progress: his playful inner child was alive and well; he had just poked his head out from his hiding place. The next step was to coax him out to play. I suggested they watch more movies so they could get more of those laughter benefits.

I also helped Roger and Jenny explore possibilities for some sexy games they could play together, games that might lead to having sex together. They agreed that they would play

"An Enchanting Evening," a board game for two that involves answering questions and touching each other a bit. The winner of the game gets to have their secret wish granted.

They came back two weeks later to announce that they had played the game...twice! The first time was awkward for Roger, and they didn't finish. He admitted to Jenny that he was afraid he might not be able to fulfill her wish if she were to win the game. After some reassurances from her, they tried the game a week later and this time enjoyed having intercourse. Jenny felt hopeful as she saw how Roger was beginning to lighten up about sex and have a little more fun. Maybe he deserved it after all!

Roger and Jenny further explored their sexual potential as Roger's inner child continued to emerge, albeit very slowly. At times, when he started to go back into hiding, Jenny would coax him out again with some comedy movies. And they continued to sample other sexy games they found online.

Fun and Games

There is an endless variety of choices for you and your partner to engage in more laughter and play. I give a smattering of ideas below. But before you jump in with the fun and games, I have a few basic pointers:

- **Competition.** A little friendly rivalry can add some pleasant tension to a game. But don't overdo it, especially for sexy games. If necessary, tone down your level of aggression so as not to overwhelm your partner. Remember, the main idea here is to connect through play, not to win at all costs.

- **Agreements.** Be clear about boundaries and respect them. If your activities involve physical contact, then do not, for example, tickle your partner mercilessly or cause pain or distress. This is about having mutual fun, not about domination (unless, of course, you are explicitly and consensually engaged in a dominant-submissive role-play scene).

- **Alcohol.** Consume alcohol in moderation. Yes, a drink or two can loosen inhibitions and feel good. But after too much imbibing, alcohol acts as a depressant. Dulling your feelings doesn't go well with laughter and play.

A good way to approach fun and games is through your inner child. Think back to your youth. What games did you love to play as a child? What made you laugh? If you have trouble accessing these memories, perhaps some of the suggestions below will spark a pleasant memory from your past.

Here are some ideas to get you started.

Laughter and Humor

- **Watch some humorous movies together**. Hollywood has great talents who love to make us laugh. Find some you like and crank up your funny bone. Standup comedy videos can be hilarious.

- **Search for "jokes" on YouTube**. There are thousands to choose from. Even the bad ones might make you laugh. (You could also search for "dirty jokes.") Maybe learn how to tell jokes. Or search for "funny videos" to enjoy some chuckles.

- **Try a few "laughter yoga" exercises** you can find online. This playful practice is a way of jump-starting the body's laughter response by forcing yourself to laugh. Once you get going, especially with a partner, a genuine and cathartic laughing fit may ensue.

- **Check out a porn website for bloopers** or outtakes and enjoy some funny moments on video. Getting a look behind the scenes of a sexy film can help you realize that pornography is simply fantasy designed for entertainment. These are actors creating a production for the enjoyment of others. It's not real life. And it's certainly not good sex education. Check out Chapter 8: Learn More about Sex for some worthwhile sex education resources.

Dance

- **Dance to music together.** It's such a great way to express yourself through your body. Slow dance to romantic crooners. Gyrate to the heavy beats of rock and roll or the sexy bass lines of funk and disco. Have fun dancing in whatever way you and your partner like. You can "dance like no one is watching"...because no one (other than your partner) will be!

- **Do a striptease for your lover.** Wear some sexy or provocative clothing, put on enticing music, and then dance seductively for your partner as you slowly remove most or all of your clothes. This can be a great prelude to sex.

Sexy Games

- **Engage in some role-playing scenarios** with your partner. Use this as an opportunity to explore unexpressed fantasies or to assume personas that might turn you on, and your partner, too. Playing a role can help you overcome shyness. You can try out some fantasies that you might not otherwise include in your lovemaking. (You'll find more details in Chapter 7: Try Something New.)

- **Try out a board game** that's based on sex or relationships, especially one that leads you and your partner to some pleasurable intimacy. I recommend "An Enchanting Evening," produced by Time for Two, which says of the game: "Spend the evening together exploring adult fantasies and desires as you roll dice and make your way around the game board and each other."

- **Play strip poker.** This can be a fun and leisurely way to get naked with your partner. All you need is a deck of cards, some rudimentary knowledge of the rules of poker, and a willingness to have some fun by shedding your inhibitions!

Unstructured Play

Engaging in play just for its own sake, without any goal in mind, is called "unstructured play." When given the chance, young kids usually love dreaming up their own activities without adult guidance or intervention. You've probably noticed how engrossed they get in simply playing. Unstructured play brings immense benefits to a child's development: self-esteem, social competence, sensory stimulation, creativity, imagination, and more.

Play is also important for adults. Play releases endorphins, improves memory, and helps us stay energetic and young at heart. I believe that play is an essential component of a healthy sex life. I encourage you to initiate some unstructured play times with your partner. These activities can be great fun and might even lead to some playful sex:

- **Have a spontaneous pillow fight**. This can be a safe way to release some aggression and get involved in physical play with your partner. Just remember, respect boundaries and don't overdo it.

- **Sing some silly songs together.** Create your own parodies of nursery rhymes. Recite naughty limericks or write some yourselves.

- **Build a blanket fort.** Transform your living room or den into your play space, and hang out there together. Watch a movie. Enjoy a meal. Pretend you're camping. You could even pitch a tent in the living room and sleep there overnight.

- **Get messy with finger paints and body painting.** This doesn't require much in the way of artistic talent, just a desire to experiment and have fun. Follow it up with a shower or bath together.

- **Soak in a bubble bath together**. Enhance the mood with scented candles and soft music. Add some sensual finger foods that you feed to each other.

If these suggestions don't trigger some ideas for you, search the internet for more possibilities.

Playful Sex

When asked about the most important characteristics in a partner, people often put sense of humor at the forefront. It's very appealing and sexy. Humor, and the playful spirit that often accompanies it, has detoxifying and defusing effects that go a long way toward keeping relationships intact.

One of the things I was surprised to learn over my years as a therapist was the high incidence of couples who do not consider sex to be a playful activity. Some view it as "serious business," like a job that needs to be completed. This attitude is often shaped by a strict upbringing or early sexual trauma.

I was fortunate enough to have a happy childhood, although it took a sad turn the day my father was killed in a car accident when I was fourteen years old. But I was resilient. I continued to forge ahead on the adventure of my life. I had already experienced a wealth of secure attachment to my playful and loving parents, and I will always be grateful for them.

Years later, once I was established in my career as a sex therapist, my mother told me how she saw my work as a logical combination of my love of people's stories and my bold—some might say brash—openness about sex. I feel so fortunate to have a profession where I can help people with such an intimate part of their lives.

Building and maintaining intimacy in a relationship takes work. And it takes courage to be vulnerable, to be intimate with another person with both your body and your innermost thoughts and feelings. But if you lay the groundwork with good communication and thoughtful attention to your partner's pleasure, a wonderland of sexual play and delight can be yours. There's a good reason the activity leading up to intercourse is often called *foreplay*!

81

I hope you find some ways to lighten up and be playful with your partner, even act silly at times. The word "silly" did not originally mean ridiculous or trivial. It comes from the Old English *saelig*, which meant prosperous, happy, and healthy. Some occasional silliness can help you enjoy all those blessings.

Chapter 7
Try Something New

I'll try anything once, twice if I like it, three times to make sure.

MAE WEST

As the saying goes, "Variety is the spice of life." You may think it a trite sentiment, but when it comes to sex, it is absolutely true. Trying something new and different in the bedroom has long been a trustworthy strategy for couples who want to relieve sexual boredom and reenergize their relationship.

For the majority of couples, the passion and infatuation of the early stages of their romance gradually fades, usually within a year or two. By then, their deepening emotional intimacy has cemented a strong relational bond, and couples often settle into a comfortable accommodation of agreeable, lowest-common-denominator sex.

But eventually, sexual boredom sets in. Surprisingly, according to research reported by Wednesday Martin in her 2018 book *Untrue*, it is women who get bored sooner, after an average of only about two years, compared to seven years for men!

The solution to boredom, of course, is novelty—something new and different. Novelty works because new experiences stimulate the release of dopamine, the neurotransmitter that acts on the nervous system to increase arousal and pleasure. It's the chemical reward signal that keeps us coming back for more.

Adding novelty turned out to be an effective strategy for Shannon and Marissa, a same-sex couple married for six years. Both women started their adult lives in a series of relationships with men before they met each other and fell in love. But their erotic life had virtually dried up. They came to see me for help in dealing with their "lesbian bed death," as this situation has been called. They wanted to rekindle the spark in their relationship but were not able to make any progress.

As I worked with this couple over several sessions, it became clear that they were stuck in a cycle of blaming each other. In the past Shannon would make sexual overtures to her partner but would routinely get rebuffed for what she considered "lame excuses." Marissa would complain that Shannon was "not doing it right," but didn't make any efforts herself.

The communication between the couple was fairly good, but they simply were stuck on the point of "who goes first." I had them complete the Sex Menu exercise from Chapter 1, but they didn't come up with anything new to try. I suggested they set up date nights, but these fell flat when their familiar squabbles arose. Then I asked if either had any sexual fantasies. At first they said no, they were just fine with the type of fairly conventional lesbian sex they had enjoyed since the beginning of their relationship. I pushed a little further and suggested that they each *pretend* that they had some fantasies, then share what those would be with each other.

With an attitude of "What do I have to lose," Marissa blurted out, "Well, I could always go back to having sex with men." There was a long moment of stunned silence in the room. Marissa continued, "I don't really want to have sex with a man, but at least it would be *something*." After another long silence Shannon said "You know, I sometimes think back to my days with men, and I enjoy some of the memories. I even get a little turned on. But I'm not really interested in having sex with a man either."

Marissa and Shannon locked eyes as if they hadn't seen each other in a long time. I suggested, "Maybe you could take turns role-playing that scenario. You know, use a strap-on to pretend that one of you is the man and just see where it leads."

They came back to the next session visibly changed. I could see much more of a glow around each of them and they showed more affection to each other now. They reported that they reluctantly tried the role-play scene, and to their surprise the sexual passion sparked between them. A few nights later they switched the roles and it worked again. They clearly expressed that they weren't interested in acting out this fantasy with a man, but the role-playing sure did the trick for them. Their case was a good example of how you sometimes have to keep digging a little deeper when seeking novel sexual inspiration.

Benefits of Novelty

Novelty offers a myriad of benefits in addition to increased sexual charge. Researchers have discovered that the desire to have new experiences—what they call "neophilia"—is positively associated with much of what helps us thrive in the world:

- **Novelty increases lifespan.** The tendency to seek new and different things naturally decreases with age. As we get older, we tend to settle into routines that are familiar and comfortable. Our resistance to change is natural...but it can lead to cognitive decline. Research shows that people who push beyond their comfort zones to try new things—even a little—live longer and enjoy greater overall health.

- **Novelty facilitates learning and boosts memory.** Our brains are naturally wired to gravitate toward new experiences. Novelty holds our attention and keeps us motivated. We also tend to have better recollection of past experiences that are novel in some way. Those who adopt an attitude of being a "lifelong learner" enjoy advantages in adaptation, resilience, and longevity.

- **Novelty counteracts depression.** I have suggested to some clients who suffer from depression that they make the commitment to seek out new places, new TV shows, new music, new food, new video games, new clothes...new anything, really. It seems to knock them out of a self-reinforcing downward spiral. Although newness is not a cure for depression, it does give folks a temporary shift in perspective from which they are better able to make more lasting, positive changes.

- **Novelty fosters personality growth.** The drive for newness, especially when coupled with the traits of persistence and self-transcendence (the ability to rise above one's limited self-centered perspective), leads to healthy personality development and happiness.

Bottom line: the adventurous spirit and curiosity evoked by novelty help keep us happy and engaged in life.

Too much novelty, however, has some downsides. A person can get hooked on seeking new experiences, which can lead to addictive behaviors or exacerbate attention disorders. The trick is to find the right balance between productive routines that make your life easier and novel events that make your life more exciting.

"I Have an Idea!"

At this point you may be asking yourself: "What's the trick to get my partner interested in using a sex toy, trying a different position for intercourse, or exploring some erotic reading or videos together?"

Navigating novelty in the bedroom is often fraught with obstacles and pitfalls, especially for long-term couples who have not experimented with novelty in a while (or ever!). The barriers you might encounter usually arise from fears or expectations:

- **Embarrassment.** If you have experienced shame about your sexuality, especially in childhood, you may be mortified to tell your partner about some secret fascination or desire. Disclosing your own eroticism to another person exposes an intimate part of yourself. Being vulnerable can also be awkward. But it may be a necessary hurdle on the path to getting what you want.

- **Concern for your partner's ego.** Perhaps you're afraid that your partner will feel "less than" if you suggest an enhancement to your lovemaking. You imagine that they might be feeling, "What? Am I not enough?" even if they don't say it.

- **Fear of rejection.** Expressing a new sexual interest involves taking a risk. What if your partner responds with a horrified look and exclaims, "You want to do *what*?!" Judgmental rejection can certainly dampen the libido. I share some ideas below about how you can guide this process to unfold more smoothly.

If you are fortunate enough to have developed good communication with your partner about your sex life, then proposing a new sexual turn-on might seem as innocent as suggesting a new restaurant for dinner. However, many people in good relationships can easily get paralyzed at the thought of talking to their partner about trying something new, especially if it carries some taboo connotations. Here are some thoughts about how you can move past these obstacles.

First, start with some baby steps. A common way that couples introduce novelty into their sex lives is the romantic weekend getaway. (However, you'll have to wait until the pandemic passes to try this one.) "Hotel sex" can be a lot hotter simply because of the newness of the setting. Sensual delights such as body pampering and fine dining also increase dopamine levels and add to the pleasure.

If you want to propose something new but aren't sure how your partner will react, try introducing the idea jokingly, as a way to gauge their interest. You could put on a sultry voice and say something like, "I think you need a spanking," or "I want to see you dressed in that," or "I want you to dress up as a _____ and do _____ to me." If your partner recoils, you can dial it back and say, "Haha! I was just kidding." No harm, no foul. But if they respond positively and begin playing along, you may find you've uncovered a whole new realm of sexy fantasies or activities to explore together.

Second, don't focus on *sexual* novelty alone. Propose some new experiences that are not related to sex. Try a new hiking trail. Play a new board game. Go for a moonlight swim. Read poetry to each other. Anything that might help boost dopamine levels for both of you. Dopamine begets more dopamine: this is another productive feedback loop, one that may get you both in the mood to be more adventurous in the bedroom.

Third, when you and your partner try something new, make a point of discussing the experience sometime afterward, no later than the next day. This is a golden moment to learn and improve. What did you like? What did you not like? How did it make you feel? How could the experience be better or different next time? This helps create new and more effective patterns of talking about sex and opens up the scope of your conversations to unexplored topics.

Finally, be direct in your statements about what you want and how you feel. If you are embarrassed, tell your partner, "I'm embarrassed to talk about this." This can help defuse your anxiety and move you along in the conversation. Don't expect your partner to pick up on subtle hints if you are too bashful about your desires. Of course, a little bit of guile can add some spice to your dance of seduction, but it's no substitute for clear and direct communication.

It's usually a good idea to talk with your partner beforehand about new things you want to try. A little planning and some agreements can help the experience feel safer. But a surprise might be fun, too. Just remember to keep it light and playful (and consensual). That way, if your surprise turns out to be unwelcome, you can both treat it as a learning experience.

Venturing into new realms of sexual activity can seem scary at first. As you dip your toes in the water, here is an important point to remember: Those tinges of fear (of embarrassment, of rejection, etc.) are actually an essential part of what drives the pleasure of novelty. Fear stimulates the release of dopamine and adrenaline, two brain chemicals also associated with sexual arousal. The ideal novel experience strikes the right balance between a manageable touch of mystery and intrigue (even danger) and a new sexual thrill that you both enjoy.

You each have your own sexual interests and preferences, and they may change over time, even with the same partner. Inviting novelty into your sexual relationship can be a way of honoring your partner's sexual desires. Couples who are able to adopt novel experiences to help satisfy each partner's needs report that they have higher levels of sexual desire and are able to maintain that desire for each other.

I am reminded of GGG—the aspiration to be Good, Giving, and Game in a sexual relationship—coined by advice columnist Dan Savage. *Good* in the sense that you are skilled in bed; "*giving* of equal time and pleasure" to your partner; and *game* "for anything—within reason." I suggest a fourth G: "Go for it!" Muster your courage and take the plunge into some new domains of passion and pleasure. You never know...it could become a habit!

So Many Choices

Oh boy! Where to begin? First of all, please know that the array of choices I present in this book—choices which include only legal activities between consenting adults—is *not* a comprehensive list. I continue to be astonished by the extensive and evolving variety of human sexual expression. People are endlessly inventive when it comes to creating ways to satisfy their sexual desires. Whether or not you see your particular turn-ons here, you can almost certainly find information (and often a community of like-minded pleasure-seekers) by searching online.

Also, don't get too hung up the particular categories of activities. A lot of these behaviors not only overlap with others but can be combined to produce a virtually endless smorgasbord of choices. One note: I have not included any information on threesomes or group sex, despite the popularity of such fantasies. The social distancing requirements of the current pandemic are not conducive to safely opening up your relationship. Of course, once the quarantines are lifted, all bets are off! (If you're interested in pursuing this, two books listed in Chapter 8—*The Ethical Slut* and *Nina Hartley's Guide to Total Sex*—offer particularly good information and guidance.)

Clients who begin to explore adding novelty to their sex lives sometimes ask me: "Am I normal?" or "Is doing this normal?" It's a reasonable question that usually stems from a person's desire to conform to societal expectations. Many of us don't want to be perceived as too eccentric or bizarre. We want to fit in. (If you must compare yourself with the general population, the book *The Normal Bar*, also listed in Chapter 8, has lots of data and details about what couples report that they actually do.)

But when it comes to private consensual behavior in the bedroom, I tell clients: forget normal. This is about you, your desires, and your unique arousal profiles. Claim your own erotic potential for fun, pleasure, and satisfaction.

Sexual Activities

If you did the Sex Menu exercise at the end of Chapter 1, then you've already got a head start on this process. If not, then I recommend you begin there. The menu lists more than forty activities—from simple hugging all the way to group sex—for you and your partner to consider. Or you can propose something else that piques your interest.

Once you choose a new activity, do some research together. In addition to searching the web, check out the how-to books and educational videos listed in Chapter 8. They include trusted resources that provide a wealth of guidance on the different techniques, positions, and activities that you could explore.

One special type of activity is erotic sensation play. This involves causing your partner to experience specific sensations in their body. You could tease them with a feather. You could blindfold them and kiss. You could rub ice cubes on their nipples. You could bite your partner's neck or claw their back. All these activities should include informed consent and agreements about boundaries. Sensation play overlaps with BDSM practices (in interlocking order: bondage/discipline, dominance/submission, and sadism/masochism—all further described below under "Kinky Play"), and together they can make a powerful combination.

Sensation play doesn't even have to be sexual. You could view it as simply another way to revitalize your senses—an extension of the sensual exercises I describe in Chapter 5. But more often than not, sensation play is a part of foreplay. It arouses the nervous system, which in turn leads to more intense and pleasurable orgasms.

Erotica

Stories and themes about sex in books, music, photography, illustration, film, and other media are strong turn-ons for many people. Depictions of sexuality have the power to excite the imagination...and the body, too! In many cases a person's first exposure to sexual media will have a strong influence on their preferences for erotic stimulation throughout their adulthood.

Erotica takes many forms in today's world. Two of the most popular genres are romance novels and pornographic films, each of which enjoys more than a billion dollars in sales in the United States every year.

The traditional "bodice ripper" themes in romance novels provide suitable titillation for many. In the last decade, *Fifty Shades of Grey* and its spinoffs—books featuring sojourns into the world of BDSM and kink—have proved riveting for a wide audience.

Side note: many sex educators and therapists point out that there are some problems with *Fifty Shades of Grey*— especially its portrayal of the power dynamics and lack of adequate consent between the two main characters. This is important because learning to use good consent practices with your sexual partners is crucial, especially when exploring edgier terrain that may push your (or your partner's) boundaries and trigger old traumas. That said, the overall impact of *Fifty Shades* has been positive, because its popularity has broadened interest in kinky sex and normalized conversations around a realm of sexual play that was previously taboo to many.

You might also check out more nuanced fiction in books such as *Ageless Erotica*, edited by Joan Price, that are geared toward a more mature audience. Search Amazon and you'll find thousands of titles appealing to all persuasions.

Porn films, of course, are the most widespread form of erotica, especially since the advent of high-speed internet connections used to stream and download videos. Pornography also engenders a lot of controversy. Some people have what may be considered legitimate concerns about the societal effects of porn. There's no doubt that many young people now get their *de facto* sex education from porn. This is regrettable since porn is really just entertainment, and the actors and actions in these films usually bear little resemblance to what a healthy sexual relationship looks like.

Another concern is the notion that porn consumption, especially by men, damages their relationships or leads to increased sexual aggression toward women. This so-called "Porn Panic" is roundly debunked by Dr. Marty Klein in his book *His Porn, Her Pain.* Drawing on scientific research about porn and his decades of experience as a sex therapist, Klein maintains—and I agree—that worry about porn usage is really a smokescreen issue that often masks more fundamental relationship problems.

I believe that watching explicit adult entertainment films with your partner can provide numerous benefits, and studies show that mutual viewing can lead to a better relationship. Of course, only do it if you both feel comfortable with this new experience. In my practice I have seen couples use "porno nights" to strengthen their sexual communication and learn more about their partner's fantasies and desires. And it can be great foreplay.

Many women, however, are not very interested in viewing the standard male-centric portrayals in most pornography. Whereas most men tend get off on the visual depictions of sex, some women would prefer sexual dramas (or comedies) that have a coherent storyline and actual character development. Enter "feminist porn." Also known as female-friendly porn, this genre has become more popular in recent years as women themselves take the reins in writing, directing, and producing these alternatives to traditional pornography. You can find standout films and filmmakers in this category at the website Feminist Porn (https://feministporn.org/). I also recommend you check out the vintage films from Femme Productions produced by the late feminist porn pioneer Candida Royalle. She was one of the first female porn stars who shifted to producing and directing explicit films featuring stories and characters appealing to women.

Sex Toys

The vast majority of sex toys (which represent a $30 billion industry!) are designed primarily to stimulate a woman's genitals and anus. The two main varieties of toys are vibrators and dildos. (Yes, of course there are vibrating dildos, too.) Usually battery-powered, vibrators create a buzzing feeling on the skin that most women find pleasurable. Female genitalia, especially the clitoris, are generally very responsive to the pulsations of a vibrator. This is why so many women use vibrators to masturbate. It feels good and often leads to orgasm quickly.

Dildos (and their anal cousins, butt plugs) are inserted to simulate penetration by an erect penis. A popular variation is the strap-on dildo, where a harness holds the dildo in place on one partner who then can use pelvic thrusting to penetrate the other person with the dildo. As you may imagine, these toys can be used on the male anatomy as well, but they are not nearly as popular with men.

How do you make the leap from masturbation to partner sex with a sex toy? Simple: show and tell. *Show* your partner how you use the toy to pleasure yourself. *Tell* your partner what it feels like. Then let your partner stimulate you with the toy. This will help your partner learn to make the right moves that turn you on. Take your time and explore all the possibilities.

For men in a heterosexual relationship, I have some pertinent advice: Make friends with the toys. I say this in response to a common situation I have encountered, where men feel threatened or intimidated by sex toys. Their thinking goes something like: "Why do you want or need a sex toy

95

except to masturbate? When we are together, shouldn't I be enough?"

If you choose to view sex toys as competition, you're missing out on some great opportunities to increase your partner's pleasure. Instead, learn how to use different toys, especially in combination with other ways to stimulate her with your mouth, your hands, and your penis. Multiple points of sexual stimulation can enhance the intensity of orgasm even more. Ask for feedback and adjust your techniques accordingly. She is likely to be very grateful for your willingness to practice and develop your new skills with sex toys. You'll get satisfaction from evoking her pleasure and receiving acknowledgement of your talents. (Plus, if you keep their batteries charged, sex toys don't experience any performance challenges, making them great friends to have at the ready.)

Furthermore, in a way, you are really no match for a vibrator. Its mechanical oscillations buzz at rates up to one hundred times per second, which produce the intense orgasmic response most women experience. Humans are physically unable to move body parts such as a finger or tongue at even a tenth of that speed. Better to treat sex toys as useful friends, even tools, that provide a technological boost to your partner's pleasure.

Dramatic Scenes

Good sex involves more than simply applying the right physical stimulation. The emotional connection between partners can play an equal (and sometimes greater) role in achieving sexual pleasure. Adding some elements of drama, such as fantasy, role playing, dirty talk, and so on, can heighten the emotions and ramp up the intensity of foreplay and orgasm.

For most of us, sexual fantasies are a normal part of our inner lives. We imagine what it would be like to experience different partners, scenarios, and sex acts. The act of fantasizing itself can be a turn-on, even in the absence of a physical stimulus. That's a testament to the power and creativity of the human mind.

Fantasy usually plays a central role in masturbation for both men and women. It's also fairly normal (and perfectly OK) for a sexual fantasy about another person to pop into your mind while you're having sex with your partner. This is not a betrayal, or "mental cheating" as one client called it. It's only your busy mind and its wandering thoughts. However, if you're bothered by your errant fantasies during sex, you might find relief by trying some of the suggestions in Chapter 3: Be Mindful about Sex.

Does having an extreme fantasy mean that you will be drawn to acting it out in real life? Certainly not. Case in point is the prevalence of rape fantasies. Studies show that a majority of people (of all genders) have fantasized about being forced to have sex. Some researchers say it is the most common sexual fantasy for women. (For men, a threesome including another woman tops the list.) Having a rape fantasy does not mean that you want to be sexually assaulted. Instead, it means that you are playing out a scenario in your own mind, on your own terms, where the sex is not really forced, but you enjoy the fantasy feeling of being forced while not having to take any responsibility for initiating sex.

Many in the sex education and advice world now prefer the term "ravishment" fantasies, to emphasize that the person being ravished, or taken forcibly, can still withdraw their consent. This is especially important to keep in mind if you and your partner ever decide to role-play such a fantasy.

In fact, we often fantasize about the things that we consider taboo, about behaving in ways opposite to our normal

97

identities, about doing things we would consider wrong or immoral in our daily lives. That's why so many women—even strong, self-assured feminists—fantasize about being ravished, and are turned on by being bossed around in the bedroom. Similarly, professional dominatrixes report that many of their clients are male executives who are required to be strong and decisive in their professional lives, but fantasize privately about giving up their power and being forced to serve someone else. Such fantasies are perfectly normal, and sharing them with your partner can be a great way to add some novelty to your relationship.

Do you ever discuss your sexual fantasies with your partner? Many people don't, usually out of fear of judgment or fear of hurting their partner's feelings. It's perfectly OK if you want to keep your thoughts to yourself. But if you're game, you might find that your fantasy life is a rich source of new and different ideas that you can leverage to spice up your real-life sex.

Sharing sexual fantasies with your partner can have pitfalls, similar to ones I discuss in the "I Have an Idea" section above. If you're unsure how either of you might react, proceed with caution and take small steps.

Sharing fantasies with your partner can have real benefits. You get to know more about your partner's turn-ons, which can guide you as you delve into more novelty together. You might find areas where your fantasies overlap, which could lead you to some new and mutually satisfying sexual experiences. Trying fantasy talk during foreplay can help jumpstart your partner's arousal. You and your partner could actively talk about a fantasy during sex, which could increase the excitement for both of you.

You might want to take a sexual fantasy to another level and role-play the scenario with your partner. You each pretend to play a different part, which can be fun and stimulating. For example, imagine that you are strangers who meet in a bar; one of you picks up the other, then you both go to a nearby hotel room for hot one-night-stand sex. Other potential scenes include driver-hitchhiker, pizza delivery guy, teacher-student, etc. Perhaps you recall playing doctor as a child. Now as a grown up you get to play like that again—this time without your clothes on!

A big advantage of having occasional role-play scenarios is that you get to act outside your normal habits and thought patterns. This could mean being more eager and less inhibited. The scenario that you enact with your partner gives each of you permission to experiment with an alter ego, a different persona who gets to do some things that you would not ordinarily consider in your usual interactions with your partner. This can be lots of fun and can lead to interesting insights about what really turns each of you on.

While you are at it, add some sexy or outrageous clothing to your scene. Provocative lingerie is often a big turn-on. Or try some fetish or kinky outfits that you think your partner might like. Perhaps you have a favorite character you would like to impersonate. It's all about having fun and getting turned on.

Another great way to add some dramatic play to your sex scenes is "talking dirty," or sexy talk. This can be a little hard to do for some people, especially if you tend to shy away from X-rated language. The talk doesn't have to be super-raunchy. A little vocal encouragement can often heat things up. Experiment to see what works best for you and your partner.

You might get turned on by the idea that a stranger is watching you have sex, or the possibility that someone catches you having sex in a semi-public location. Surveys show that this level of exhibitionism appeals to about 20% of adults. It could be as simple as leaving the bedroom window shades partially open. Of course, your options may be limited by social distancing during the pandemic, but a fantasy about making love outdoors or in a restroom stall could provide some extra pizzazz.

Kinky Play

Lastly, I have a few comments about options from the world of kink, which is generally used as a catch-all phrase for nonconventional sexual practices. People drawn to this arena are said to have a bend or "kink" in their sensual or sexual proclivities that sets them apart from the world of straight or "vanilla" sex.

Kinky play can be quite diverse and does not necessarily involve being sexual. A large subset of kink is BDSM, which stands for bondage and discipline, dominance and submission, sadism and masochism. BDSM activities range from light restraints and spanking all the way to elaborate rope bondage and domination...and much, much more. The Wikipedia entry for "Glossary of BDSM" lists more than one hundred terms!

You may wonder why someone would be drawn to a sexual scenario that focuses on the intentional infliction of pain or humiliation. It turns out that some people are just wired that way. They derive pleasure from their own particular experience of feeling pain, or they find satisfaction from acts of submission or domination. A person's particular kinks are often shaped by their specific childhood experiences.

If kinky activities interest you, I recommend you do some research online before you jump in. The website Kink Academy (www.kinkacademy.com) is a good place to start. It offers a comprehensive library of sex-ed videos and online courses for adventurous, consenting adults. Kinky play often involves one partner assuming a dominant role and the other playing the submissive, which works well for role playing.

Since some activities border on the physically dangerous, it can be a good idea to connect with a local community of kinksters to "learn the ropes."

The kink community places a strong emphasis on communication, consent, boundaries, and aftercare, since these elements are necessary for the participants' safety. These values are also important for all sexual encounters, regardless of the presence of kinky activities. These precepts are a welcome and useful contribution to the field of sexual health.

Chapter 8
Learn More about Sex

An investment in knowledge pays the best interest.

BENJAMIN FRANKLIN

Knowledge is power. Did you know that people who have more sexual knowledge are more confident in their sexual conduct? Confidence in bed is also a huge turn-on for many people. If you and your partner find yourselves with more free time than usual during quarantine, why not use it as an opportunity to broaden and deepen what you know about sex?

Whether you are a sexual novice or a master lover, one of the joys of being human is that there is always more to learn. In this chapter, I'll guide you to a range of resources—books, films, educational videos, podcasts, and websites—that you can access to learn more about sexual topics while you and your partner are in living in lockdown...and beyond.

Instead of binge-watching shows on Netflix or playing video games, I recommend that you use some of your time to expand your range of knowledge and get better at the things you already know. There is a plethora of options and activities listed here to help you learn more—ranging from books addressing the anatomy, psychology, and history of sex; to instructional videos about all kinds of techniques; to entertaining relationship advice podcasts; to interactive online courses.

Over the past thirty years, I've collected hundreds of books and videos about sex. Many creators of these works have been guests on my *Love, Lust, and Laughter* online radio show, hosted on Progressive Radio Network. Below are some of the best, most trusted resources I've found. (You'll find links under Resources at my Web site at www.DearDrDiana.com).

Books

How-To Sex Guides

Guide to Getting It On: Unzipped
Paul Joannides

This is the first book I recommend to my clients. It's possibly the best book ever written about sex. This comprehensive book is a fun read, filled with entertaining illustrations and detailed, hands-on information about all kinds of sexual practices. I have a PhD in Human Sexuality, I've worked more than thirty years as a sex therapist, and I've also had a lot of sexual experience...and I still learned a lot from Paul's guide. Rolling Stone Magazine called it "the only sex manual you'll ever need!"

Great Sex: A Man's Guide to the Secret Principles of Total-Body Sex
Michael Castleman

Michael Castleman is the nation's top journalist specializing in men's sexuality. Learn from this excellent guide and your partner will sing your sexual praises. Also, check out Michael's popular "All about Sex" blog on www.psychologytoday.com, and look for his forthcoming book Great Sex Guidance. You can hear several conversations with Michael in the archives of my Love, Lust, and Laughter program.

Nina Hartley's Guide to Total Sex
Nina Hartley

This is a well-written and wide-ranging tour of the varieties of sexual activities that humans engage in, with lots of practical how-to information. In addition to chapters on the basics (foreplay, oral sex, intercourse), the book includes sections on toys, threesomes, BDSM play, and more. Nina Hartley has performed in more than a thousand porn films in a career spanning more than three decades, so she knows what she's talking about. Her enduring star power is complemented by her articulate work as a sex educator.

Succulent SexCraft: Your Hands-On Guide to Erotic Play and Practice
Sheri Winston and Carl Frankel

Do you dream of becoming an erotic virtuoso? You'll find answers in Sheri and Carl's visionary, practical guide to whole and empowered sex. In my favorite chapter, Sheri spells out "The Six P's of Touch": PRESENCE: Be present. Touch here now. PURPOSE: Hold a positive intention. PATIENCE: Don't rush; take your time. PRECISION: Be accurate and focused. (Body painting each other can be a fun game!) PATTERN: Think musically and artistically—use rhythm, themes and motifs. PROGRESSION: Keep it moving and coherent. Follow Sheri's tips for more playful sex so that you can develop your own "sexcraft" toolkit.

The Sex & Pleasure Book: Good Vibrations Guide to Great Sex for Everyone
Carol Queen, PhD, with Shar Rednour

This book draws on the vast and diverse experience of the customers of Good Vibrations, the legendary feminist adult toy store founded in San Francisco in 1977. Back then the store made waves with its focus on sex education and women's pleasure. Today, Dr. Carol Queen is the Good Vibrations Staff Sexologist. She is extremely knowledgeable—informing and inspiring sexual comfort and exploration.

She Comes First: The Thinking Man's Guide to Pleasuring a Woman
Ian Kerner, PhD

As the book jacket says, most men are "ill-cliterate"—totally ignorant about what lies under the hood of a woman's clitoris, let alone what to do with it to facilitate her pleasure. Unfortunately, far too many women don't understand their own anatomy, either. And even if they do, they're conditioned by society to prioritize men's pleasure and settle for a lifetime of unsatisfying sex. This book demystifies the vulva and offers dozens of practical tips to help her come...and keep her coming back for more!

Better Sex through Mindfulness: How Women Can Cultivate Desire
Lori A. Brotto, PhD

Mindfulness is essential for good sex (as I detail in Chapter 3 of this book). You've got to stay in the moment. That's easier said than done these days, even when there's no pandemic to contend with. Dr. Lori Brotto has pioneered the use of mindfulness in treating sexual problems—helping thousands of women to overcome issues such as low desire or arousal, and to have more and better sex.

Come as You Are: The Surprising New Science That Will Transform Your Sex Life
Emily Nagoski, PhD

The author, a researcher focused on women's well-being, discusses her experiences working with women who wonder: "Am I normal?" (Spoiler alert: the answer is almost always yes.) In this vital work based on recent breakthroughs in brain science, Nagoski dispels many of the myths about female sexual arousal. Through entertaining vignettes of four women struggling to make their arousal cycles work for them, this book provides practical advice on navigating common libido responses to stress, mood, and trust.

Sexual Intelligence: What We Really Want from Sex—and How to Get It
Marty Klein, PhD

What do we really want from sex? In this book, sex therapist and Psychology Today columnist Marty Klein delves deep into the whys and hows of sexual arousal and desire, explaining that shifting how you think about sex is far more important than anything you actually do in the bedroom.

The Big O: How to Have Them, Give Them, and Keep Them Coming
Lou Paget

All bodies come equipped with the tools for orgasm, yet without proper education and opportunities to practice, many people never successfully achieve the synergy of mind, body, and spirit needed to release this unique and revelatory experience. Lou Paget, a sex researcher and author of eight books, shows everyone, regardless of your gender or equipment, how to bring your partner to high sexual delights and delicious orgasms.

The Sexy Little Book of Sex Games: Surprise Your Lover with Sensual Playtime
Ava Cadell, PhD

Sex is play. Too many couples forget that. As I detail in Chapter 6, maintaining a sense of playfulness and fun is one of the keys to a healthy relationship. Ava Cadell's fun little book is full of ideas to help you spice things up with your lover, including tips for sexy foreplay, erotic foods, dirty talk, sensual massage, fantasy role-playing games, and more.

Sex and Relationships

Mating In Captivity: Unlocking Erotic Intelligence
Esther Perel

New York-based psychotherapist Esther Perel highlights the central issue that plagues every long-term relationship: the tension between our needs for safety and security on the one hand, and novelty and freedom on the other. In other words, the longer we spend together with a partner, the more secure we feel in a relationship, but the more we tend to get bored, to lose the sense of mystery and discovery that drew us together in the first place...and the more likely we are to stray outside the relationship in search of novelty and freedom. Using examples from her own therapy practice, Perel offers practical ways you can regain and maintain that sense of novelty and mystery, and see your partner again with new eyes. Required reading for every long-term couple.

Passionate Marriage: Keeping Love and Intimacy Alive in Committed Relationships
David Schnarch, PhD

Differentiation is the cornerstone theory of Passionate Marriage. Differentiation involves learning to balance your individuality (separateness) with your emotional connection to someone else (togetherness). Standing on your own two feet—rather than trying to merge with your partner or lose yourself in love—may lead to the best sex you've ever had. "Sex gets better, not worse, as you get older," declares Schnarch. "Great sex is not about how your body looks or how you position it. It's about your frame of mind and emotional connection with your partner."

Love Worth Making: How to Have Ridiculously Great Sex in a Long-lasting Relationship
Stephen Snyder, MD

Can erotic love last? Yes, says my friend Stephen Snyder. And in his latest book, the good doctor shows you how. Over his three-decade career as a psychiatrist focused on relationships and sex therapy, he has worked with more than 1,500 patients. Dr. Snyder has collected a wealth of practical insights into what it takes for couples to maintain a healthy sexual connection. Read this sensible guide to learn the hidden rules for great sex.

21 Decisions for Great Sex and a Happy Relationship
Lori Buckley, PhD

Decisions, decisions. Whether you realize it or not, you are constantly making choices that affect yourself and the people around you—especially your romantic partner. This short book by Dr. Lori Buckley, a frequent guest on my online radio show, gives practical guidance to help you envision your ideal relationship and empower you to make more mindful, conscious decisions to move toward that goal.

The Erotic Mind: Unlocking the Inner Sources of Passion and Fulfillment
Jack Morin, PhD

Written in 1980, The Erotic Mind is a foundational work in the sexual literary canon. Author Jack Morin interviewed more than a thousand people, asking participants to describe their peak sexual experiences and fantasies, and discovered some surprising commonalities. He turned these findings—that anger, guilt and anxiety can powerfully affect our libidos—into a simple formula for tapping into your desires: attraction + obstacles = excitement.

The Heart of Desire: Keys to the Pleasures of Love
Stella Resnick, PhD

How do you keep love and lust alive in a long-term relationship? The key, according to Stella Resnick (a longtime friend and mentor of mine and author of the definitive The Pleasure Zone), is to prioritize pleasure and playfulness. This excellent book includes Dr. Stella's 10-Step Loving Sex Program, a practical method for deepening your sense of intimacy and erotic connection.

The Way of the Superior Man
David Deida

This classic text offers practical lessons for men struggling to navigate the perennial challenges of women, work, and sexual desire. "It is time to evolve beyond the macho jerk ideal, all spine and no heart," Deida writes. "It is also time to evolve beyond the sensitive and caring wimp ideal, all heart and no spine." This book provides powerful insights that can help any man tap into his sense of purpose to be more passionate, caring, and grounded in all realms of life and relationships.

9 Secrets to Bedroom Bliss: Exploring the Sexual Archetypes to Reveal Your Lover's Passions and Discover What Turns You On
James Herriot, PhD, and Oona Mourier, PhD

There's more than one way to be a great lover. You could be any one of the nine sexual archetypes so skillfully described by these authors. Are you an Innocent? An Adventurer? A Revealer? A Nurturer? Delve into your archetype and explore some juicy exercises to strengthen your best qualities. This framework is also a great tool for understanding and healing sexual incompatibilities.

Sex at Dawn: How We Mate, Why We Stray, and What It Means for Modern Relationships
Christopher Ryan and Cacilda Jethá

According to our standard cultural narrative, the dominant relationship model—long-term monogamous coupling—is not only morally right, it's determined by evolution. Authors Ryan and Jethá turn that narrative on its head, utilizing recent findings in anthropology, archaeology, primatology, evolution, and psychobiology to make the case that monogamy is actually a recent development in human history: it has been common only since the widespread adoption of agriculture about 5,000 years ago. Before that, they argue, humans evolved for tens of thousands of years in nomadic tribal groups where survival required extreme cooperation and sharing of everything—from food to child rearing to sexual partners. They explore how these insights into our evolution from promiscuous apes can help us better understand our desires and navigate modern relationships with less stress and shame.

Untrue: Why Nearly Everything We Believe about Women, Lust, and Infidelity is Wrong and How the New Science Can Set Us Free
Wednesday Martin, PhD

According to conventional wisdom, men are horny cheating dogs and women are the faithful ones. In reality, says Wednesday Martin, women are even more likely than men to desire sex with multiple partners. And they are increasingly more likely to act on that urge. Recent studies show that women tend to get bored of sex with a single partner after just one to two years, while men take an average of seven years to reach that point. The growing interest in consensual nonmonogamy (open or "monogamish" relationships, polyamory, swinging, etc.) is driven more by women than by their male partners.

The Seven Principles for Making Marriage Work: A Practical Guide from the Country's Foremost Relationship Expert
John Gottman, PhD and Nan Silver

Relationship researchers John and Julie Gottman are famed for their discovery that, based on the ratio of a couple's positive and negative interactions, the psychologists can predict whether a marriage will end in divorce with 94% accuracy. Anything less than four positive statements for every negative one and the marriage is in serious trouble. This book is the culmination of their findings from 35 years of research at their Seattle "Love Lab" into what makes relationships succeed or fail. Gottman describes the warning signs and provides exercises to help you rebuild your friendship and intimacy with your partner.

Sex Without Stress: A Couple's Guide to Overcoming Disappointment, Avoidance & Pressure
Jessa Zimmerman
This book focuses on a common pattern that arises in relationships: the sexual avoidance cycle. Based on her years of experience helping couples navigate this pattern, sex therapist Jessa Zimmerman has developed a nine-phase experiential process to help identify your own negative patterns and implement solutions to break those cycles. This book will help you communicate your desires more effectively and shift your mindset around intimacy in your relationship.

Practical Science & Health

The Science of Orgasm
Barry Komisaruk, PhD, Carlos Beyer-Flores, PhD, and Beverly Whipple, PhD
This is a geeky guide full of fascinating details about how the human body actually produces all those pleasurable sensations of sex. If deciphering a mix of neurotransmitters, hormones, and physiological changes like vasodilation is your thing, you'll come away from this well-written book with a better appreciation of the complex workings of sexual response.

Why We Love: The Nature and Chemistry of Romantic Love
Helen Fisher, PhD
Romantic passion is not an emotion. It's a primal need as powerful as hunger, hardwired over millions of years of evolution. So says renowned anthropologist Helen Fisher in this fascinating exploration of her research into the brains of people who had recently fallen madly in love. Romantic love

113

is also universal. Fisher found that people feel equally passionate about their new loves, regardless of factors like nationality, age, race, religion, gender, sexual orientation, or economic status.

Bonk! The Curious Coupling of Science and Sex
Mary Roach

Mary Roach brings humor and curiosity to her exploration of how scientists do research on our favorite subject. Bonk! is an anthology of some of the most wacky and interesting sex research projects to grace the halls of academia. Roach unveils the many ways sex researchers have been shamed for attempting to share their knowledge with the general public. We also learn how they've tried to answer that age-old question: "What do women want?" If you enjoy science and history mixed with a lot of laughter, this is a great resource on how we know what we know (and don't know) about human sexuality.

Love Sense: The Revolutionary New Science of Romantic Relationships
Sue Johnson, EdD

Why do humans feel the need for long-term romantic partners? According to Sue Johnson (bestselling author of Hold Me Tight), we evolved to form deep, loving bonds as a survival strategy, similar to the need for secure attachment between a mother and child. Johnson delves into the emerging research on attachment psychology and explains what you can do to foster a healthy, secure bond with your mate.

The Normal Bar: The Surprising Secrets of Happy Couples and What They Reveal about Creating a New Normal in Your Relationship
Chrisanna Northrup, Pepper Schwartz, PhD, and James Witte, PhD

How do you find out what's normal in sex and relationships? You team up one wellness entrepreneur with two PhD sociologists, who then survey more than 100,000 people around the world about their intimate lives. The Normal Bar summarizes those findings with insights about sexual frequency, positions, foreplay, kissing, money, cheating, obsessions, kinky sex, and much more. The authors include suggested exercises that readers can use with their partners to address a range of relationship issues.

The Vagina Bible: The Vulva and the Vagina— Separating the Myth from the Medicine
Jennifer Gunter, MD

Gynecologist Jennifer Gunter wrote this comprehensive guide to the vulva to help women (and men) separate fact from myth about one of the least-understood parts of the human body. The book starts with an anatomical overview of the purposes and amazing features of each part of a woman's genital anatomy. Gunter then moves into a systematic review of the various myths and harmful products that have been marketed to fix problems that don't exist, and provides practical solutions to common problems that do exist. This is a user's manual for anyone who has a vagina or comes into regular contact with them.

Ultimate Guide to Male Sexual Health: How to Stay Vital at Any Age
Dudley Seth Danoff, MD

Good information, like a good man, is hard to find. Dr. Dudley Seth Danoff, MD, offers abundant, accurate information in this wide-ranging book, such as: super foods to invigorate your sex life, the health benefits of having sex, important questions a gay man should ask his doc, and ways to stay sexy as you age. Danoff is a world-renowned urologist whose message is: at its finest, great sex is an emotional connection that combines good skills backed by informed knowledge.

Special Topics

The Ethical Slut: A Practical Guide to Polyamory, Open Relationships, and Other Freedoms in Sex and Love
Janet W. Hardy and Dossie Easton

Let's face it, most humans are not very good at monogamy. Just look at the rates of infidelity and divorce. But if you've ever cheated on (or been cheated on by) a partner, you know that the pain and heartache is typically about the deceit and loss of trust, not the sex act itself. Authors Hardy and Easton show us how to claim our wandering nature, communicate our desires with our partners openly and honestly, and live more exciting and fulfilling sex lives.

His Porn, Her Pain: Confronting America's PornPanic with Honest Talk about Sex
Marty Klein, PhD

We sex therapists frequently hear female clients complain about their husband's "porn addiction." The reality, according to Marty Klein, is that excessive porn use is not itself a problem, but can be an indicator that there are deeper relationship issues that may need work. This book unpacks many of the myths around pornography and the adult entertainment industry. Klein details how, in the absence of quality sex education, teens turn to porn for information about sex. He recounts how right-wing Christians and sex-negative feminists formed an unholy alliance against the porn industry. And he offers a prescription for Americans to heal our unhealthy relationship with porn through more open and honest talk about sex.

Naked at Our Age: Talking Out Loud about Senior Sex
Joan Price

Joan Price is on a mission to dispel the myth that older people are not interested in sex. She writes about expanding our ideas of what sex is, exploring and celebrating sexual pleasure, enjoying orgasms with or without a partner, and navigating responsive desire. The book is filled with tips and advice from experts, including Yours Truly. This guide provides everything for the over-sixty set to live a more fulfilling and sensual lives.

Divorce with Decency: The Complete How-To Handbook and Survivor's Guide to the Legal, Emotional, Economic, and Social Issues
Bradley A. Coates, Esq.

Sex is one of the three main causes of divorce. (The others are money and family.) According to long-time divorce lawyer Brad Coates, another frequent guest on my radio show, "in divorce situations there has been either too much sex outside the marriage, or too little within it." If you're considering ending your marriage, this important book might actually help prevent it from getting to that point.

Simple Sexy Food: 101 Tasty Aphrodisiac Recipes and Sensual Tips to Stir Your Libido and Feed Your Love

Linda De Villers, PhD

Oysters, strawberries, pistachio nuts, papayas, ginseng. Every culture has foods that it considers aphrodisiac. And cooking aphrodisiac foods together is a great way for you and your partner to enjoy some sensual fun that just might get you horny. As I wrote in the Foreword, this book is "practical, inspiring, erotic, and elegant." It's also the only cookbook I know of that was created by a certified sex therapist. Each recipe includes fun facts about the aphrodisiac history of that particular dish.

Videos and Movies

OMGyes

https://www.omgyes.com/

Despite decades of research into the biology, psychology, and sociology of sex, until recently no one had ever done a large-scale study on the mechanics of the female orgasm. Enter OMGyes. The website, which features explicit videos of real peoples' experiences, was launched in 2016. It disseminates practical information based on the findings of a peer-reviewed study of over 2,000 women, ages 18-95, looking at what actually makes women come. And now they have great suggestions for couples, too. Check out their "Inner Pleasure Collection."

Sex Smart Films
www.sexsmartfilms.com

This "Netflix of Sex Education" is an online library featuring a wide variety of more than 600 films about all aspects of sexuality. Curated by my friend, sex educator and filmmaker Mark Schoen, the site features all six of the educational videos that I wrote and narrated, including "How to Seduce Your Lover Forever."

Better Sex Video Series
Sinclair Institute
www.bettersex.com

One of the most popular series of instructional videos, the Sinclair Institute's Better Sex programs have helped millions of people overcome their inhibitions and expand their sexual repertoires. We learn so much visually! This is sex education at its best, and many of my clients have praised the videos. They feature commentary by sex experts and explicit depictions of real couples having sex, and cover many topics including tantric positions, advanced oral sex, fantasy role-playing, and tips for incorporating sex toys into partnered sex. My most recent Sinclair narration was for "Great Sex for a Lifetime," Volumes 1 and 2.

SmartAss Productions Expert Guides Series
Tristan Taormino, director
https://puckerup.com/feminist-porn/tristans-films/expert-guide-series/

Ever since *Fifty Shades of Grey* became a smash hit, interest in the kinkier options on the sexual menu has soared. For couples interested dipping their toes—and other body parts—into this territory, the Expert Guides video series by sex educator and feminist pornographer Tristan Taormino is a great place to start. The series includes guides to female ejaculation, pegging, advanced fellatio and cunnilingus, rough sex, anal pleasure, and more.

Masters of Sex

This hit Showtime series is based on the biography of famed sex researchers William Masters and Virginia Johnson. Between 1956 and 1969, the pair conducted research into human sexuality at Washington University in St. Louis. The show explores both their pioneering work and their personal relationship, which boldly challenged cultural and academic boundaries in a tumultuous time in American history. Side note: I had the pleasure of serving on a panel with Dr. Masters and Dr. Ruth Westheimer (another giant in our field), in Washington, DC, in 1995, talking about sex and aging.

While You Were Gone: The Untold Story of Candida Royalle

Alternate title: **Candice**
Sheona McDonald, director
https://whileyouweregonefilm.wordpress.com/about/
or https://www.candicemovie.com/

This 2019 documentary tells the life story of Candice Vadala, better known as Candida Royalle. Acknowledged as the godmother of feminist porn, Royalle started her career as a porn star in the 1970s, at the height of the sexual revolution. In 1984 she began making her own films, breaking with industry norms by focusing on women's pleasure. Candice was a personal friend of mine for over twenty years before her untimely death from ovarian cancer in 2015. This touching film tells the inspiring story of this beautiful and complex woman.

Podcasts

Savage Lovecast
Dan Savage
https://www.savagelovecast.com/
One of the most popular sex and relationships podcasts on the internet, this weekly show is hosted by the often-irreverent advice columnist Dan Savage. It's full of great tips for navigating modern relationships, mixed with entertaining political and cultural commentary. Savage answers questions from callers of all ages, genders, sexual orientations, and relationship styles. No topic is taboo. Calls and answers range from online dating tips to polyamory; from BDSM to talking about your relationships with family. Every episode features an interview with a guest expert, often sex researchers discovering new insights about what turns us on and why.

Sex with Emily
Emily Morse
http://sexwithemily.com/
Emily Morse is on a crusade: "Saving the world, one orgasm at a time." A pioneer in sex advice podcasting, she's been at it for more than ten years. And somehow, she keeps pumping out three episodes a week of intelligent, entertaining, and compassionate advice to listeners around the world. She also hosts a daily satellite radio show on SiriusXM and writes numerous articles on topics from sex toy reviews to mutual masturbation; from ethical porn to sex-positive parenting. With its massive searchable archive of hundreds of podcast episodes, articles, and blog posts, her website is practically an encyclopedia of great sex advice.

Sex Out Loud
Tristan Taormino
https://www.pleasurepodcasts.com/sexoutloud

If you're curious about some of the edgier realms of sex, this weekly show by powerhouse Tristan Taormino is a great place to start. For decades she has been a sex educator, author, feminist pornographer, and activist for sexual freedom. Each episode features an in-depth interview with a guest expert on a wide range of topics, including sex in pop culture, anal sex, kink, sexual politics, erotic literature, trans rights, consensual nonmonogamy, and many more. Her relaxed yet enthusiastic style makes it entertaining and fun to learn about topics that may be a little uncomfortable for the uninitiated.

Bawdy Storytelling
https://bawdystorytelling.com/podcast

If you like NPR's The Moth, you'll love this podcast. Hosted by "sexual folklorist" Dixie De La Tour, each ten-minute episode features sexy and entertaining personal tales told at live monthly story slams around the United States by poets, writers, burlesque performers, comedians, scientists, teachers, sex workers, and just plain folk. Since the pandemic began, the monthly Bawdy story slams have gone online. Tune into the livestream on a date night for some fun, sexy entertainment that'll get you and your mate in the mood. And the show's archive of 100+ episodes is available online for free.

Pleasure Podcasts
http://pleasurepodcasts.com

To expand your podcast menu even further, explore the Pleasure Podcasts network. This family of smart, sexy, funny shows includes Sex Out Loud and Bawdy Storytelling, plus eight other podcasts that explore sex and relationships from many different angles. One fun option is Sex Talk with My Mom, a weekly conversation between a 30-something male comedian and his 60-something cougar mother, in which they discuss their dating lives and dispense relationship advice to listeners.

Online Resources

Sex and Psychology
Justin Lehmiller, PhD
www.lehmiller.com
Tap into the mind of psychologist Justin Lehmiller, PhD, one of the country's top sex researchers. On his personal blog, he gives us a regular glimpse into how he and his colleagues at the University of Indiana's famed Kinsey Institute are expanding the frontiers of knowledge with their research into the science of human sexuality.

Psychology Today Blogs
https://www.psychologytoday.com/us/blog/
The website of the venerable magazine Psychology Today is home to a wealth of blogs and columns offering expert information and advice on sex and psychology. Contributors include Michael Castleman, Paul Joannides, Marty Klein, Justin Lehmiller, and dozens more.

Sexual Intelligence Blog
Marty Klein, PhD
https://www.martyklein.com/
Another of my favorite blogs comes from Marty Klein— therapist, author of five books, educator, and expert on sex in the media and public policy. He shares strong and intelligent

opinions on controversial topics including porn, censorship, sexual diversity, and more. Subscribe free to his blog newsletter.

Kink Academy
https://www.kinkacademy.com/
Whether you're just beginning to explore the kinkier side of sex, or looking to master your advanced techniques, Kink Academy is a comprehensive resource offering hundreds of online courses led by their faculty of dozens of experienced kinksters.

Chapter 9
Express Gratitude

Let us be grateful to the people who make us happy; they are the charming gardeners who make our souls blossom.

MARCEL PROUST

After being isolated with your partner at home for a few weeks (or months), expressing gratitude may not be the first thing on your mind. You may be stressed out from coping with the messy realities of close-quarter, day-to-day life.

It's easy for small annoyances to build up and then burst forth in displays of anger and frustration. It's almost inevitable under these circumstances. After all, you didn't ask to be stuck in the middle of a pandemic indefinitely.

Learning to deal with these irritations is key to a successful sequestration. My advice is twofold. First, find simple ways to defuse the tension through better communication and reasonable compromise with your partner. Second, make a diligent, daily effort to express more gratitude for the fortunate things in your life, especially your beloved partner.

Defusing the tension can be as simple as remembering to use the Deep Listening exercise from Chapter 1. This can help clear up any miscommunication causing the conflict. Another trick is to take three deep breaths when you first feel the urge to criticize your partner. After breathing deeply, ask yourself: "Is this issue really worth bringing up right now? Is there a different way to deal with this that would serve us better?"

So, to rephrase my first piece of advice above: Cool it with the criticism during quarantine. Practice some ways to manage your frustrations and moderate your reactivity. If you and your partner have what seem like major issues to deal with, you'll probably be better off postponing those discussions until you can get more time away from each other and gain a better perspective on your relationship.

My second piece of advice is to practice gratitude. While you are spending lots of time together, a great way to counteract your frustrations and tensions is to focus on what is good, and then verbally announce your appreciation. Numerous studies have shown that expressing gratitude confers a wealth of benefits on your physical and mental well-being.

Benefits of Gratitude

Gratitude is the freely-given expression of thanks and appreciation for someone or something. Psychologists and neuroscientists have been studying its effects for decades, sometimes by comparing one group that has a regular gratitude practice to another group that doesn't. In addition to measurable increases in the brain's levels of the beneficial neurotransmitters dopamine and serotonin, here are some of the many benefits experienced by those who practice gratitude:

- Better sleep
- Reduced stress

- Fewer aches and pains
- Increased happiness
- Less depression
- Higher self-esteem
- More robust psychological resilience
- Enhanced empathy and lowered aggression
- Diminished toxic emotions, including resentment and frustration
- Help in overcoming trauma
- Opportunities for new relationships
- Increased energy and productivity

Wow! What's not to like about gratitude? This is why I so strongly encourage you to start expressing thankfulness more often. It's an easy, simple, and surprisingly effective survival strategy for your relationship during this time in quarantine—and any time, really.

The truth is, many relationships suffer from emotional undernourishment. People forget to say what they value and appreciate about their partner. This was the case with Janet and Cameron, a couple I worked with not long ago. They came to see me after Janet discovered that Cameron had been having an affair with another woman. He ended the affair and they both took steps to repair their marriage, which neither of them wanted to end.

As we explored the reasons that Cameron sought sex outside of his marriage, we gradually uncovered some underlying patterns in their communication that needed work. Janet was not overly critical, but she was hesitant to give Cameron much appreciation. She had fallen into a rut of complacency that is quite common among long-term couples. For his part, Cameron had a hard time saying what he really wanted, mostly out of fear of rejection.

I suggested they try the Sweet Nothings exercise described below. It's basically Eye Gazing (from Chapter 1), but with verbal expressions of love and gratitude. When Janet and Cameron first tried this, they each had trouble finding things to say. I encouraged them to keep at it. If you don't have a habit of being thankful, it can take some time to build up your gratitude muscles.

After a few more attempts they had a breakthrough. They did the exercise in my office and Janet told Cameron that she was thankful for his attentiveness to her when they have sex. He had never heard a compliment like this before from Janet. He was so touched that he began to cry in this tender and vulnerable moment. It seems he had been waiting for years to hear this kind of validation from her. (We all later came to understand that seeking validation was part of what drove him, albeit unconsciously, to have an affair.)

Janet and Cameron slowly opened up to more and more things they appreciated about each other, and Cameron got better at expressing his needs. When I saw next, they had created a new foundation on which they continued to rebuild their marriage.

Gratitude Exercises

What are you grateful for? It could be almost anything: your health, your financial situation, your partner, your children, your extended family, your career. Of course, this is not a perfect world. There are likely some aspects of your life you would like to see improve. But I suggest you set those aside for now. You can work on them at another time.

The idea here and now, while you are confined to home, is to focus on the positive. With a little practice, you can create a self-reinforcing cycle of appreciation between you and your partner. When you experience the pleasant feelings caused by the gratitude-induced release of dopamine and serotonin, your brain will naturally motivate you to seek more of those rewards. The more you're grateful, the better you feel. The better you feel, the more you have to be grateful for. Before you know it, you've initiated a positive feedback loop that boosts your overall sense of well-being.

I've included below some short gratitude exercises to consider incorporating into your daily routine. Making gratitude a consistent practice—even a *habit*—is essential to achieving the beneficial results. It's not important which of these exercises you use. What's important is that you *actually use some of them!*

Since these are partner exercises, I recommend you focus on expressing gratitude to and for your partner. The more you do these exercises, the more you'll find that expressing appreciation becomes second nature. But in the meantime, the exercises are a great way to get started. Try them out. Be creative and adapt them to your needs or circumstances. It's well worth the effort.

There is no magical secret to expressing gratitude. You simply tell the other person what you like and appreciate about them. It's easy to start with appreciations of your partner's *actions*, such as, "Thanks for making coffee for me this morning." I recommend that you look for opportunities to also comment about your partner's *character*, such as "You're so thoughtful." This helps your partner to feel truly seen and valued, and (bonus!) it engenders further thoughtful actions. There's that positive feedback loop.

To top it off, you can punctuate your expression of gratitude by adding how glad you are to be the *recipient* of your partner's thoughtfulness. "Thanks for making coffee for me this morning. You're so thoughtful. I'm very lucky to be with you!"

What if you don't find anything to be grateful for? That's OK: the process of searching for something to be grateful for is helpful in itself. Plus, it activates your mind to begin to notice more positives in your partner.

And don't forget to thank your partner even for the small things. If the words "thank you" and "you're welcome" are not already a frequent part of your daily vocabulary, they should be.

Sweet Nothings Exercise

This is similar to the Eye Gazing exercise in Chapter 1, where you sit facing each other. In this case you'll talk, telling each other *sweet nothings,* those words of affection exchanged by lovers. I suggest you begin with the phrase, "What I love about you is (fill in the blank)." For example, "What I love about you is the sound of your voice." Or, "What I love about you is your sense of style." Or, "What I love about you is the way you moan and purr when I massage your shoulders."

Set a timer so each person can share for two minutes, with no interruptions. Gaze into your partner's eyes. Start each sentence with, "What I love about you is..." and then complete the sentence. Continue with more sentences and more things you love about your partner. Don't overthink it, just let it flow. If you get stuck searching for something to say, just say, "What I love about you is...everything!"

Keep going until your turn is up. The listener should just listen, and maybe smile or nod their head, but should not speak until the end of the two minutes. When the speaker's time is up, the listener should smile and say something like,

"Thank you," or "You are very observant." Then reset the timer and change roles, so that the first listener now speaks and the other partner listens.

One thing to notice during this exercise: Do you have trouble accepting or believing some of the things that your partner says they love about you? For some people, sincere compliments—much less true expressions of love from a partner—can be difficult to receive. It's important not to negate anything your partner says about you. At the end of the exercise, do not downplay or minimize any positive qualities your partner sees in you. Simply accept the compliments in the moment. If they cause any issues for you, find some other time when you can process your feelings of self-doubt.

Take note: the Sweet Nothings exercise can be very powerful. It can evoke strong emotions, especially for a person who has felt deprived of this kind of acknowledgement in the past. It's not unusual to shed tears and comfort each other during this exercise. Savor the tender moments as treasured keepsakes for your relationship. At other times, this exercise can be an energizing prelude to a lovemaking session.

Gratitude Journal Exercise

If you enjoy writing, keep a journal of your thoughts of gratitude. Putting words to paper (or computer screen) can be therapeutic. It can also help you clarify what's really dear to your heart. It can reveal patterns of your expressions of gratitude over time. Nurture a self-reinforcing cycle of appreciation that blossoms between you and your partner. You'll likely notice that you're feeling better and better with each passing day.

Surprise Love Notes Exercise

Put a sticky note in the kitchen cupboard that says, "World's Sexiest Cook." Use lipstick to write, "You're HOT!" on the bathroom mirror. Leave a note partially hidden under your partner's keyboard that reads, "I love all the special things you do for me...and to me." You get the idea. Have some fun leaving little gratitude gifts around the house for your partner to discover.

Bedtime Gratitude Ritual Exercise

Just before one of you drifts off to sleep, take a moment to recount at least one thing that happened that day that made you feel grateful for your partner. It's a comforting way to end the day and doing this will help you get a better night's sleep.

Gratitude and Sex

One of the strongest core emotions in humans is the need to be loved, to be cherished...to be desired by another. However, sometimes the complex dance of relationship obscures this fundamental drive. You may lose connection with the spark that drew you together in the first place. Yet the desire is still there, lurking in the shadows, just waiting to be reclaimed.

Expressing gratitude in the form of *compliments* can open the doorway to that desire. All of us—men and women alike—enjoy being told that we are attractive. When you compliment your partner's desirability, it tends to arouse *their* desire as well. Let your partner wholeheartedly know how and why they turn you on. This type of gratitude can trigger a positive feedback loop of desire and desirability, helping to rekindle the stirrings of your initial attraction to each other.

Being vulnerable with each other as you express your true desires helps build trust. It helps you feel validated and appreciated on a deeper level. It gives you a secure foundation so that you can safely let go and surrender to the ecstasy of sexual passion.

Can you imagine yourself saying (or hearing) something like this? "Wow, I sure appreciated all that hot sex last night. You are such a skilled lover. I'm very lucky to be with you."

Building this kind of intimacy and weaving it together with passionate sexuality can be a lifetime project. On this journey with your partner, you can have the time of your life!

Chapter 10:
Recommit to Your Relationship

Life loves to be taken by the lapels and told: I am with you, kid.
Let's go.

MAYA ANGELOU

In the midst of the uncertainties surrounding the coronavirus pandemic, it is natural for our priorities to get reordered. Things like social distancing, hand washing, sanitizers, face masks, and even toilet paper(!) occupy more of our thoughts than usual and lead us to radically change some of our daily activities.

It's also stressful learning new behaviors, such as attending a Zoom meeting, ordering groceries online, homeschooling your kids, or cohabitating with your partner 24/7 in a confined space. Most people don't like change, and it can be a major source of anxiety.

The material I have presented in this book—the exercises, the suggested activities, the insights into the psychology of couples—are all designed to help you cope with these changes. My wish is that some of these offerings will help you better manage your stress and anxiety, and ultimately strengthen your relationship.

But these techniques can only go so far. The fact remains that we are all caught up in a life-and-death drama unfolding on the world stage as well as in our own neighborhoods and families. This fact, and our inability to do much about it other than stay home, is at the core of a certain existential angst. Will I die? Will some of my friends or family die? What about the potential for economic devastation? How are things going to be different once the immediate danger passes (whenever that will be)?

If you're feeling this angst, you are not alone. Social media memes remind us that "we are all in this together." But if you are stuck at home with your partner, you may in fact *feel* very alone. Alone with your fears about what the future may bring.

These fears of loss—sometimes called anticipatory grief— are very real. They can be debilitating and can seem very scary. But I'm here to remind you that you have a choice about how you react to this collective grief. On the one hand, you can let yourself become overwhelmed with worry and feelings of helplessness, in which case you'll need to focus much of your energy on just maintaining some sense of sanity.

But on the other hand, you can choose to leverage this grief into a heartfelt desire to really embrace your own *aliveness* today. Fear of loss? Fear of death? Yes! Move into those fears to discover what really matters to you. The question, "What am I afraid of losing?" is another way of asking, "What makes my life worth living?"

Perhaps it has been a while since you've had such a discussion with your partner, or even had these kinds of thoughts at all. This pandemic can serve as an excellent opportunity to reexamine and clarify your values. Sit down with your partner and share your hopes and dreams. Be specific about the losses you have experienced and those you anticipate. Use the fears engendered by the pandemic to strengthen the bond with your beloved and to live a more authentic life, a life that is truer to the values you hold dear.

COVID-19 can be your wake-up call about your own mortality. Work with your partner to get clear about your priorities, both for yourself and for the two of you together. Use this time to review where you are and make a renewed commitment to moving forward together in a healthy way.

The physical and emotional power of sex—this raw and sublime connection to the essence of the human life force—can elevate us into rarefied realms of ecstasy...and beyond. When your passion for sex, your lust for life, and your desire for meaning converge, a goldmine of pleasure and satisfaction awaits.

Having been a sex therapist for most of my career, I naturally tend to view people and events through the lens of sexuality. As I said in the Introduction, I see myself as a "cheerleader for great sex." So, in that spirit, I offer some options below on how you might find insights about life and relationship through your own sexual experiences.

The Meaning of Sex

Here's a quotation from a favorite author of mine, David Schnarch, PhD:

> What makes human sexuality quintessentially human is our ability to bring meaning to sex. Reaching your sexual potential involves creating transcendent meanings through profound intimacy, eroticism, and passion.

Schnarch is a big fan of *differentiation*, a mature psychological state wherein you stay true to yourself while also staying connected to your partner. Differentiation opens the doors to self-discovery and erotic expression, especially in a committed relationship. You and your partner get to explore the pleasurable possibilities together to find profound meanings for yourselves.

A good place to start is with this question: Why do you want to have sex? Have you ever thoroughly examined your own underlying sexual motives? Researchers have found that there are lots of different reasons people give for having sex. Here's a top ten list, in alphabetical order:

Reasons for Having Sex

_____ Accomplishment

_____ Affection

_____ Bargaining/Exchange

_____ Communication

_____ Concern for Partner

_____ Duty/Obligation

_____ Procreation

_____ Recreation/Play

_____ Spiritual Bond

_____ Tension Release

How would you rate these reasons in order of importance for you, and then for you and your partner? Take a moment to copy this list down in a journal, then number the items from 1 to 10, with 1 as the most important. There's no right or wrong order: they're just your preferences, like your favorite color. Some may have no meaning at all for you. Or you may have other reasons that don't appear on this list. The idea here is to tease out the "why" regarding your urges to be sexual.

Did you give a top rating to Recreation/Play or Affection? This indicates that you may find meaning through various forms of sensual exploration. Were Concern for Partner or Duty/Obligation high on your list? In that case, you might find meaning in the high moral standards of your behavior. If you chose Bargaining/Exchange or Communication, perhaps you revel in the thrill of erotic intimacy that two people can generate.

Use this list as a springboard for discussion with your partner. It's just a tool, a starting point that can lead you to deeper knowledge and understanding of each other. Pay special attention to those transcendent meanings that stir your body and touch your soul.

Pandemic Sex

One question I have asked myself is, "What significance could a couple derive from having sex during a pandemic?" To answer, think back to the 9/11 terrorist attacks in 2001, which marked the last time a major catastrophe completely captured our national attention for a dramatic and extended period of time. There is some truth to the claim that this pandemic is the "new 9/11." But rather than occurring as a single event, the coronavirus has spread like an invisible wave across seemingly random locations. And similar to 9/11, its direct consequences will continue for a long time.

Our circumstances are different in 2020, but many of the psychological effects are the same: trauma, fear, uncertainty, grief. People responded in 2001 with tremendous outpourings of emotion and compassion for the losses we suffered.

People also responded by having more sex. In the article "Perhaps the Most Primal Post-Disaster Reaction: Sex," which appeared in the October 1, 2001 edition of *The Los Angeles Times*, author Kathleen Kelleher recounts stories of people, especially in New York City, who were drawn to having "end-of-the-world sex" as a means to cope with "terrifying feelings of fear, vulnerability and sadness."

When we share an intense traumatic event—whether terrorist attack or virus pandemic—our emotional defenses get scrambled. We are more fearful and vulnerable to strong feelings, which may energize our primal sex drive. This is a key reason so many servicemen in World War II got married shortly before going overseas. They thought that might be their last chance to experience sex.

There are biological underpinnings for this phenomenon of post-disaster sex. Experiencing fear and feelings of sexual arousal each cause you to breathe more heavily as your pulse rate increases and adrenaline courses through your body. Fear also stimulates the release of dopamine and testosterone as a way to prime your body for a fight-or-flight response. These two powerful neurotransmitters also stimulate the libido and motivate you to seek pleasurable rewards. A similar dynamic is at play when a couple has intense "make-up sex" right after a heated argument, when anger causes a physical response much like that of fear.

Consider using the concept of "pandemic sex" to your advantage. Could you imagine harnessing the energy of fear to create deeper and more poignant intimacy with your partner? Could you be vulnerable enough to express your fears of loss in the midst of sexual passion? Could you be confident enough to trust your partner with your innermost essence? Could you be compassionate enough to let your inner child surrender to the pleasure of the moment?

Seven Secrets

I would like to end this book with some special advice. I call these tips the Seven Secrets for Sensational Sex—the kind of sex that keeps you curious about what's going to happen next, and keeps you coming back for more.

My husband Bryan and I developed these guidelines over the course of our now almost ten-year love affair. The secrets are simple, and they can help you continue to evolve toward your sexual potential. Plus, you'll have lots of fun and pleasure along the way.

Dr. Diana's Seven Secrets for Sensational Sex

1. Take Care of Yourself First. This means taking responsibility for your own well-being during a sexual encounter. If something hurts, say so. If something is happening that you don't like, say so. Don't assume that your partner will know these things. If you each make a commitment to speak up for yourselves, it frees up both of you to be more present. Neither partner has to be overly concerned about the other, because you trust that your partner will tell you if there's a problem.

2. Respect Boundaries. This is essential for creating and maintaining a safe "container" when the two of you are engaged in sex. If your partner has told you that a certain activity or body part is off limits, then simply don't go there. "No" means No. Of course, you're always free to renegotiate boundaries, but have that conversation at another time.

3. Communicate Openly and Directly. Don't play games or be coy when you are communicating something important about sex with your partner. Don't hold back or use vague language. It pays to be open and direct. If you have trouble talking about sex, revisit some of the guidance I shared in Chapter 1.

4. Don't Take Anything Personally. A common response when we hear rejection or criticism is to become defensive, which can be a real buzzkill in a moment of passion. Assume the best about your partner's intentions and, if necessary, act on their feedback. If a comment does strike a defensive chord with you, resolve to address the issue at another time. Chances are, the comment is not really about you but is instead a reflection of something else that may be bothering your partner. (Of course, if the comment is about something that hurts or feels bad, then stop doing what you were doing.)

5. Focus on Your Partner's Pleasure. Some sex therapists advise clients to focus on their own pleasure first. This approach has some merits, in the sense that you are the one having the experience in your own body, and thus you know best what feels good. But if each partner remains engrossed in their own pleasure, sex can devolve into little more than mutual masturbation. You would be missing out on the wonders of pleasuring each other, which can set up positive feedback loops of sensual delights and intimate connection. My husband's motto is: "Worship your woman and the Goddess will reward you!"

6. Express Gratitude. This secret is so important that I devoted all of the previous chapter to the topic. But don't limit your expressions of gratitude to exercises or daily rituals. Tell your partner how much you appreciate their actions in the moment when you are enjoying sex together. It's another way to generate a positive feedback loop!

7. Let Go. The first six secrets help establish a physically safe and psychologically healthy environment, which allows you to abandon yourself to the throes of passion. Surrendering control in the moment opens the doors to higher levels of pleasure and ecstasy where you can explore the promised land of your sexual potential.

Here again is the list of my Seven Secrets:

1. Take Care of Yourself First

2. Respect Boundaries

3. Communicate Openly and Directly

4. Don't Take Anything Personally

5. Focus on Your Partner's Pleasure

6. Express Gratitude

7. Let Go

I encourage you to practice these principles with your partner. They can serve as simple touchstones to guide you in the process of finding deeper meaning as you recommit to the intimacy and sexual abundance of your relationship.

May these secrets guide you and your partner to newfound depths of love in the time of corona.

Epilogue

B y the time you reach this page, it is quite possible that the "time of corona" may have subsided or even passed. Here in the spring of 2020, no one can say with much certainty how events may unfold.

What I know is that the spread of this novel coronavirus, and the deadly COVID-19 disease it causes, is sure to have enormous economic and medical consequences for years to come. Equally tragic is the toll on the mental health of so many people who are stressed and anxious about all the losses suffered in this pandemic.

My goal has been to equip you with some tools to counteract your stress and alleviate your anxiety. I sincerely hope that you and your partner have benefited from at least some of the advice, exercises, stories, and other information I have shared in this book. Couples who take advantage of this time to open up to more sensual and sexual connection with each other are creating a firm foundation for their future.

I also know that the material in this book can benefit couples beyond the time that quarantines are lifted. You don't need a pandemic to reclaim your birthright to pleasure. It's there for you to choose in any moment. May you continue to deepen your intimacy, strengthen the bonds of your relationship, and, of course, have fun!

Perhaps in the years ahead you and your partner will look back upon 2020 and fondly recall when you rekindled your love in the time of corona.

If you asked me why I came to this Earth,
I will tell you: I came to live out loud.

EMILE ZOLA

About the Author

Dr. Diana Wiley, PhD, has practiced for more than thirty years as a licensed marriage and family therapist, a board-certified sex therapist, and a gerontologist. Since 2010 she has hosted the online radio show "Love, Lust, and Laughter" on Progressive Radio Network. Dr. Diana has published two studies in medical journals on aging and sexuality and was appointed as a Clinton Presidential Delegate to the 1995 White House Conference on Aging, where she was the only delegate to speak about love and sexuality. (Fun fact: Dr. Diana and Bill Clinton dated over the course of several years in college days, and they remain friends today.)

Dr. Diana has given lectures and presentations on Aging and Sexuality in Amsterdam, Paris, Spain, Japan, and India at the World Congress(es) of Sexology, and at many US conferences, mainly at meetings of The Society for the Scientific Study of Sexuality. Before going to graduate school in 1979, Dr. Diana worked as an English teacher in Hawaii, Italy, and Mexico City. She also worked as a fashion model and performed on stage and in film productions in New York, Los Angeles, Miami Beach, and Honolulu.

For more information and ongoing advice, visit www.DearDrDiana.com.

Made in the USA
Monee, IL
05 June 2020